BILLIONAIRES MIND

"I knew that if I failed I wouldn't regret that, but I knew the one thing I might regret is not trying."

-Jeff Bezos, founder and CEO Amazon

Blueprint of Entrepreneurship

Vivek Choudhary

Dedicated to

The Entire Entrepreneur

Hope This Blueprint Will Guide You to Success

PREFACE

"Your work is going to fill a large part of your life, and the only way to be truly satisfied is to do what you believe is great work. And the only way to do great work is to love what you do."

— *Steve Jobs*

Entrepreneurs are the world of business and they also focus on the important drive and factors of development. They are the symbol of business achievement as well as they are well known for leadership, management, research and development, innovation, and creation of a business. Thus it is the integrated approach and integrated concept of the high amount of opportunities. Entrepreneurs start their business for some kind of profit and they start a business to share some kind of information and to increase the revenue. They possess risk with various sources such as competitors, market, financial, and other risks. These risks and skills create opportunities for growth and revenue. The mission of the entrepreneur is not only to be competitive but also to be superior high quality and world-class in order to get acceptance.

Most people work for a company or an organization, under the guidance of a boss or a leader. But there are a few who have the courage and the vision to start their own business and work for no one but themselves. Such people are called entrepreneurs. Unlike the stability of working for a reputed company, being an entrepreneur involves lots of investment risks. Getting the capital investment, setting up the operation, defining processes, and breaking even - these are the major steps that every entrepreneur has to undergo before making a profit and being deemed successful by society.

The entrepreneurial journey is not as simple as this is presented in the picture. The first thing that you will need is a business plan with which you will try to predict your journey in the most detailed pieces.

I always used to dream to become an entrepreneur, as I completed MBA and got the job, but still, I was not satisfied, I believe that I can do better, tomorrow will be more beautiful than today, this is not what I belong to, I had a big dream to have multiple businesses as my hero is Warren Buffett, so I learn from this blueprint, my passion is business and value investing, The day I quit the job, I was unemployed and searching for a good opportunity to start a venture and wondering, how can I solve the problem so that customer can buy my product. Entrepreneurship is a journey, in this journey, you will get up and downs, so ready to enjoy your journey, there is nothing call destination, every day there will be something new to learn, from one business to multiple businesses.

INTRODUCTION

Concept of entrepreneurship. Basically, entrepreneurship is the process that a person identifies a new opportunities for setting up an enterprise to make their dream come true. While an entrepreneur is the one willing to take the risk to start up a business in order to make a profit. There are many people who misunderstand that a successful entrepreneur is born. In fact, is opposite, an entrepreneur can be trained to learn entrepreneurial knowledge and skills such as managerial skills, marketing skills, and entrepreneurial attitude. Courage, tenacity, innovative, risk-taker are some of the characteristics of a successful entrepreneur. There are many real-life successful entrepreneurs example such as Steve Jobs, Bill Gates, so on. Therefore, with all those necessary skills, knowledge, and characteristics everyone could be one of them in the future!

In this book you will learn about the blueprint of entrepreneurship, in this framework, we have Opportunity, People, and Finance.

- How to find the right Opportunity
- How to Solve the Problem
- Whom to test your Product
- How to build your Team
- How to raise capital

Learn from the blueprint of most successful entrepreneurs like Bill Gates, Elon Musk, Jack Ma, Mark Zuckerberg, J. K. Rowling, Warren Buffett, Charlie Munger, Jeff Bezos, Henry Ford, and Thomas Edison.

Most people never take the first step because they are too worried about not being good enough, not having enough experience, or how people will perceive them during the journey. Trust me, if you worry about all that and never start, you'll never be great – you'll never achieve that dream of yours to start a business. Step out of your comfort zone.

You will read about the blueprint of Entrepreneurship, how do they raise money and manage risk, how do they develop a product idea, how they build the right team and scale the company, how they create a barrier to entry, economic moat, how do they succeed and those who fail, if the venture fails, what could be the exit plan, how to find a right investor and what kind of term sheet require to build a successful company.

You will learn how to identify the opportunity and test the idea. How to manage a start-up venture, help you to understand how the entrepreneurship ecosystem work, how you can solve the problem, and create a successful venture.

By the end of the book, I hope you will be comfortable enough to use the effective tool of blueprint in your venture and build a successful company. Let start the entrepreneurship journey..

About the Author

Vivek Choudhary is a Value Investor & Entrepreneur who has over 20 years of experience in investment and entrepreneurship. Involve in diversify business Commodities, Manufacturing, Hotel & Automobiles.

He earned MBA in finance & Marketing at IIPM, MDP in Strategic Market Planning at IIM, Equity Research Analyst at BSE Institute, Value Investing at Stanford University Continue studies, and Entrepreneurship Essential & Leading with Finance at HBX Harvard Business School & Value Investing at

Columbia Business School, Business Lesson Cohort at Harvard Business School Online.

He is passionate about Value Investing and invests globally. His hobby is reading. Every day he read value investing books and finance books.

He admires his Hero Mr. Warren Buffett Chief Executive Officer of Berkshire Hathaway – He follows his footprint of Value Investing. For him reading and studying are like compounding, it will help him in achieving his passion.

He wrote the book

- **Value Investing & Behavioral Finance**

- **Wealth Creation & Financial Statement Analysis "Dream to be Wealthy"**

- **Value Investing - Legendary Graham & Dodd Valuation**

- **Value Investing CHECKLIST**

- **Billionaires Mind – Blue Print of Entrepreneurship**

- **Why Investors Fail**

www.security-analysis.com

CONTENTS

Preface   III

Introduction   V

ENTREPRENEURSHIP

1. Introduction to Entrepreneurship   2
2. Benefits to be Entrepreneur   15
3. Statistics of Entrepreneurship   30
4. Why Entrepreneur Fail   38
5. Lesson from an Entrepreneur   43
6. Mindset of an Entrepreneur   54
7. Blueprint of Entrepreneurship   60
   - Opportunity   69
   - Calculate total market size   84
   - Create Competitive Advantage   89
   - Create Economic Moat   93
   - The End Point   98
   - Right People   101
   - Financial Analysis   109
   - Monetary value   112
   - Net Present Value   114
   - Internal Rate of Return   116
   - Value of Your Investment   124
   - Why the venture Fail   128

CONTENTS

- Free Cash Flow — 131
- Cash Conversion Cycle (CCC) — 140
- Burn Rate & Fume date — 143
- Source of funding — 156
- Three Rules to make — 155

BLUEPRINT OF BILLIONAIRES MIND

8. Steve Jobs — 165
9. Warren Buffett — 174
10. Charlie Munger — 185
11. Henry Ford — 191
12. Oprah Winfrey — 197
13. Jeff Bezos — 205
14. Bill Gates — 211
15. Thomas Edison — 218
16. J.K. Rowling — 223
17. Sam Walton — 231
18. Arnold Schwarzenegger — 237
19. Jack Ma — 243
20. Elon Musk — 250
21. Mark Zuckerberg — 257

ENTREPRENEURSHIP

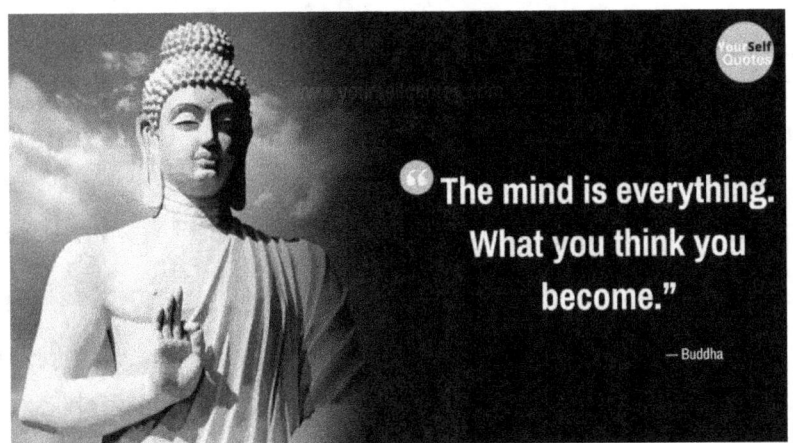

1
Introduction to Entrepreneurship

Entrepreneurship can broadly be defined as the creation or extraction of value. With this definition, entrepreneurship is viewed as change, which may include other values than simply economic ones.

Some more narrow definitions has described entrepreneurship as the process of designing, launching and running a new business, which is often initially a small business, or as the "capacity and willingness to develop, organize and manage a business venture along with any of its risks to make a profit."The people who create these businesses are often referred to as entrepreneurs. While definitions of entrepreneurship typically focus on the launching and running of businesses, due to the high risks involved in launching a start-up, a significant proportion of start-up businesses have to close due to "lack of funding, bad business decisions, an economic crisis, lack of market demand, or a combination of all of these."

A somewhat broader definition of the term is sometimes used, especially in the field of economics. In this usage, an entrepreneur is an entity which has the ability to find and act upon opportunities to translate inventions or technologies into products and services: "The entrepreneur is able to recognize the commercial potential of the invention and organize the capital, talent, and other resources that turn an invention into a commercially viable innovation." In this sense, the term "entrepreneurship" also captures innovative activities on the part of established firms, in addition to similar activities on the part of new businesses. Yet, the definition is still narrow in the sense that it still focuses on the creation of economic (commercial) value. Entrepreneurship is the practice of forming a new business or commercial enterprise, usually in an industry or sector of the economy with a large capacity for growth. Entrepreneurship is generally synonymous with resourcefulness, ingenuity, and the ability to take calculated risks in order to introduce a new, untested product or service into the marketplace. These traits are often referred to collectively as the "entrepreneurial spirit."

Entrepreneurship is driven by the entrepreneur, a person who launches and oversees the operations of a new business venture. The entrepreneur is generally self-employed, self-motivated, and ambitious and is willing to take chances to meet his or her goals. Unlike the capitalist, a businessperson who generally limits his or her role to financing commercial ventures, the entrepreneur is the driving force behind the formation of a new business and asserts a great deal of control over the key management decisions. Many entrepreneurs also assume responsibility for hiring and managing employees. Successful entrepreneurs tend to be highly skilled at organizing and motivating their employees.

In some cases the entrepreneur invents or develops a new product or service, which then forms the core of his or her new business. In other cases, however, the entrepreneur simply discovers a new way to market and sell an existing product or service. The risks undertaken by the entrepreneur are often considerable. Some entrepreneurs invest everything they own into their new enterprise, with no guarantee that the business will succeed. Other times a successful businessman will risk his reputation on a new idea, the failure of which could potentially jeopardize his entire career. Because of the high level of risk involved in entrepreneurial endeavours, the entrepreneur generally hopes to earn a high rate of return in the venture.

According to many twentieth-century economists, entrepreneurship is an indispensable aspect of capitalism. Capitalism is an economic system characterized by free markets (situations in which goods and services are bought and sold, with competition determining the prices), private or corporate ownership of the means of producing and distributing goods and services, and minimal government regulation of business practices. In a capitalist economy prosperity is driven by economic growth. Entrepreneurship helps promote such growth by continually providing the economy with new ideas that ultimately lead to more efficient and profitable business models.

While qualities of entrepreneurship have undoubtedly played an important role in business innovation since the earliest days of commerce, the concept of entrepreneurship is relatively new. According to economic historian Fritz Redlich (1892–1978), entrepreneurship first emerged in the sixteenth century, when German military officers regularly recruited mercenaries for armed expeditions throughout Europe. In Redlich's view, these recruiters exhibited many of the qualities of the modern business entrepreneur, demonstrating a willingness to take great risks in travelling into hostile territories and embarking on dangerous military campaigns.

The word entrepreneur was first introduced by the Franco-Irish economist Richard Cantillon (1680–1734), who coined the term in his landmark work Essay on the Nature of Commerce in General . Although Cantillon wrote the book just before his death in 1734, it was not published until 1755. In the early nineteenth century French political economist Jean-Baptiste Say (1767–1832) was among the first to argue that the entrepreneur played an indispensable role in promoting economic growth.

The writings of British political economist and philosopher John Stuart Mill (1806–73) brought the word entrepreneur into popular use. Like Jean-Baptiste Say, Mill viewed the entrepreneur as a dynamic force in business innovation. Mill's contemporaries, however, felt that the concept of entrepreneurship was at odds with classical economics (a theory asserting that economies were driven by markets rather than individuals). As a result, the importance of entrepreneurship was downplayed by most mainstream economic thinkers of Mill's time.

In modern capitalism, entrepreneurship found its most fertile breeding ground in nineteenth-century America. A number of significant factors contributed to the emergence of the entrepreneur in the early decades of the United States. For one, the American sense of national identity, rooted in qualities of personal freedom, independence, and a strong work ethic, proved highly conducive to the rise of the entrepreneurial individual. At the same time, the ready availability of raw materials in the United States, combined with the nation's large geographical size and rapidly expanding population, provided the resources and the potential markets for long-term economic growth. Furthermore, the federal government imposed few regulations on private business and allowed liberal access to the nation's natural resources. All of these circumstances led to the rise of enterprising, ambitious entrepreneurs who, rather than feeling overwhelmed by the challenges of building a new national economy, viewed the seemingly limitless potential for growth as an unprecedented opportunity.

One of the most important American entrepreneurs of the late nineteenth century was the Scottish-born steel magnate Andrew Carnegie (1835–1919). The epitome of the "self-made man," Carnegie rose from humble origins to become one of the wealthiest and most powerful businessmen in America. He embodied many of the essential characteristics of the entrepreneur. Hardworking and friendly, Carnegie impressed his early employers with his dedication, intelligence, and ambition, qualities that earned him rapid advancement at an early age. He was also fiercely dedicated to self-improvement, and throughout his life he strove to educate himself on a range of subjects, from economics and business to literature and art.

In many ways, the story of Carnegie's success is representative of the entrepreneurial ideal. At age 16 he began working as a messenger for a telegraph office and quickly earned a series of promotions, becoming superintendent of the Pittsburgh branch of the Pennsylvania Railroad Company before he was 20. Although his pay was modest, Carnegie soon began making shrewd investments, eventually earning enough capital to begin investing in larger, more lucrative businesses, such as oil and steel. By the 1870s he had purchased his first steel mill in Braddock, Pennsylvania; numerous other steel mill purchases followed, and in 1892 he formed the Carnegie Steel Company, which soon became the most profitable corporate entity in the world. In 1901 he sold his steel holdings and devoted the rest of his life to philanthropic pursuits.

By the early twentieth century economists had begun to develop more sophisticated theories of entrepreneurship. In his book The Theory of Economic Development (1912), Austrian economist Joseph Schumpeter argued that creativity, initiative, and risk taking, all key characteristics of the entrepreneurial enterprise, were essential to technological innovation and economic growth. Schumpeter's writings proved influential, and as a result the entrepreneur took on far greater significance in twentieth-century economic theory. In his early work Schumpeter emphasized the role of the individual who possessed unternehmergeist ("entrepreneurial spirit") in driving innovation. Later he focused on the entrepreneurial aspects of the corporation, arguing that the solitary entrepreneur was being replaced by corporate research and development departments, in which groups of individuals collaborated to develop new business ideas.

Later in the twentieth century a number of economists, notably American Frank H. Knight (1885–1972) and Austrian-born Peter Drucker (1909–2005), tried to quantify the role of innovation and risk in defining the modern entrepreneur. In Knight's view the risk associated with entrepreneurship was primarily calculated and controlled, and the entrepreneur's decision-making process was greatly informed both by his or her own past business experience and by close analysis of diverse business models. Knight argued that the successful entrepreneur paid careful attention to the laws of probability (the likelihood of a particular event occurring) in assessing the risk of a particular business decision. In his book Innovation and Entrepreneurship (1985), Drucker examined forms of entrepreneurship that focused less on technological advances and more on discovering new ways to market existing products and services. In Drucker's view the quintessential entrepreneur was Ray Kroc (1902–84), the founder of McDonald's, who transformed a single hamburger restaurant into an internationally branded chain. Drucker also asserted that the characteristics of the successful entrepreneur were not innate to the unique individual but rather were traits that most people could study and learn to adopt.

Entrepreneurship is an act of being an entrepreneur, or "the owner or manager of a business enterprise who, by risk and initiative, attempts to make profits". Entrepreneurs act as managers and oversee the launch and growth of an enterprise. Entrepreneurship is the process by which either an individual or a team identifies a business opportunity and acquires and deploys the necessary resources required for its exploitation. Early-19th-century French economist Jean-Baptiste Say provided a broad definition of entrepreneurship, saying that it "shifts economic resources out of an area of lower and into an area of higher productivity and greater yield". Entrepreneurs create something new, something different—they change or transmute values. Regardless of the firm size, big or small, they can partake in entrepreneurship opportunities. The opportunity to become an entrepreneur requires four criteria. First, there must be opportunities or situations to recombine resources to generate profit. Second, entrepreneurship requires differences between people, such as preferential access to certain individuals or the ability to recognize information about opportunities. Third, taking on risk is a necessity. Fourth, the entrepreneurial process requires the organization of people and resources.

The entrepreneur is a factor in and the study of entrepreneurship reaches back to the work of Richard Cantillon and Adam Smith in the late 17th and early 18th centuries. However, entrepreneurship was largely ignored theoretically until the late 19th and early 20th centuries and empirically until a profound resurgence in business and economics since the late 1970s. In the 20th century, the understanding of entrepreneurship owes much to the work of economist Joseph Schumpeter in the 1930s and other Austrian economists such as Carl Menger, Ludwig von Mises and Friedrich von Hayek. According to Schumpeter, an entrepreneur is a person who is willing and able to convert a new idea or invention into a successful innovation. Entrepreneurship employs what Schumpeter called "the gale of creative destruction" to replace in whole or in part inferior innovations across markets and industries, simultaneously creating new products including new business models. In this way, creative destruction is largely responsible for the dynamism of industries and long-run economic growth. The supposition that entrepreneurship leads to economic growth is an interpretation of the residual in endogenous growth theory and as such is hotly debated in academic economics. An alternative description posited by Israel Kirzner suggests that the majority of innovations may be much more incremental improvements such as the replacement of paper with plastic in the making of drinking straws.

The exploitation of entrepreneurial opportunities may include:

- Developing a business plan.
- Hiring the human resources.
- Acquiring financial and material resources.
- Providing leadership.

- Being responsible for both the venture's success or failure.
- Risk aversion.

Traits of an Entrepreneur:

- He is the person who develops and owns his own.
- He is the moderate risk taker and works under uncertainty for achieving the goals..
- He is innovative.
- He peruses the deviant.
- Reflects strong urge to be independent.
- Persistently tries to do something better.
- Dissatisfied with routine activities.
- Prepared to withstand the hard life.
- Determined but patient.
- Exhibits sense of leadership.
- Takes personal responsibility.
- Oriented towards the future.
- Convert a situation into an opportunity.
- Tends to continue in the face of difficulty.
- Also, exhibits the sense of competitiveness.

A Few Questions to Ask Yourself:

- *Do I have the personality, temperament, and mindset of taking on the world on my own terms?*

- *Do I have the required ambiance and resources to devote all my time to my venture?*

- *Do I have an exit plan ready with a clearly defined timeline in case my venture does not work?*

- *Do I have a concrete plan for next "x" number of months or will I face challenges midway due to family, financial or other commitments? Do I have a mitigation plan for those challenges?*

- *Do I have the required network to seek help and advice as needed?*

- *Have I identified and built bridges with experienced mentors to learn from their expertise?*

- *Have I prepared the rough draft of a complete risk assessment, including dependencies on external factors?*

- *Have I realistically assessed the potential of my offering and how it will figure in the existing market?*

- *If my offering is going to replace an existing product in the market, how will my competitors react?*

- *To keep my offering secure, will it make sense to get a patent? Do I have the capacity to wait that long?*

- *Have I identified my target customer base for the initial phase? Do I have scalability plans ready for larger markets?*

- Have I identified sales and distribution channels?

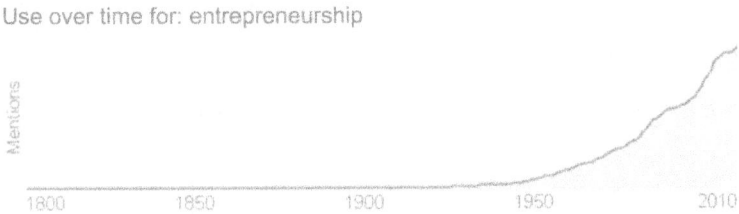

Think about it: 100 years ago, what options did an entrepreneur have? If you didn't have the skill to make something, and didn't have the capital to buy something, you were out of luck. Fast forward to today, and there be 582 million entrepreneurs in the world.

It often involves great risk and uncertainty, but it's also an opportunity to overcome those challenges and manage multiple aspects of a business operation. From marketing to accounting to logistics and beyond, entrepreneurs oversee the many facets of running a business.

But entrepreneurship isn't easy. In fact, data shows that 90% of startups fail. Despite this, entrepreneurship remains an extremely enticing career path. Like many high-risk activities, it often draws people who see the risks as an exciting challenge rather than a disclaimer.

And while the risk might be great, so are the rewards — entrepreneurship is easily one of the most creative and rewarding forms of business. And some of the most well-known people across the world are famous entrepreneurs, including Oprah Winfrey, Bill Gates, Walt Disney, J.K. Rowling, and Steve Jobs.

If you aspire to be like these successful people, entrepreneurship might be the path for you.

2
Benefits to be an Entrepreneur

Entrepreneurship can feel like a tedious and intimidating process at times — however, the rewards of entrepreneurship are so great they're worth your hard work and time. Let's take a look at some of the specific benefits of entrepreneurship.

- You control your destiny — you're in charge of your business, goals, mission, and more.

- You manage your schedule including how and where you're going to spend your time.

- You're your own boss and manage all aspects of your business the way you see fit.

- You feel motivated to succeed, grow, and come to work — you believe in what you do.

- Your life is exciting — every day is filled with new opportunities to grow, develop your skills, and learn.

- You decide who you'll bring onto your team as you grow (if and when you choose to expand your team).

- You determine your salary based on your efforts and the success of your business.

- You feel a sense of reward and motivation you most likely won't feel in any other position, at any other company.

- You can change the world for the better — you'll inspire others to pursue their dreams, create a product or service to solve a community's (or group's) needs.

- Implementing an Idea

    Perhaps you have come up with an idea for a product or service that no one else has thought of and can make people's lives easier. By putting your idea to work by starting a business, your idea may help people, while giving you the chance to earn a substantial income.

- Pursuing a Passion

    You may be a creative person who is working in a "non-creative" career. For example, an accountant may be truly an artist or writer at heart. By becoming an entrepreneur, you can pursue these types of careers on a freelance basis. If you prefer, you can even pursue your passion part-time until you are able to generate a full-time income.

- You set your own schedule

    Though entrepreneurship can often require long hours, the benefit of building a business is that you are in charge of deciding when you want to work. Instead of the monotonous 9-5 set-up, you're able to have more independence and freedom. It's not that you are doing less work, but rather that you're able to choose when you want to work in order to accommodate other activities in your life.

- You believe in what you do

    Working in entrepreneurship is inspiring. Instead of being a cog in the wheel for a giant, hierarchical corporation, you are able to see your ideas make a difference and contribute to the construction of a brand new business.

- Your workplace can vary

    Don't expect to always be working from inside an office while working for or creating your own start-up. Entrepreneurs and other start-up founders often work from home or while traveling, instead of within an office. The ability to opt out of working constantly in an office is a great way to be able to experience a change in scenery and break up the monotony of always working in the same space.

- You're the boss

    You have a large degree of agency and control in what's happening when you're starting your own company. You get to build a team, decide where the company is going, and call the shots.

- You get to see your work change lives

    Part of what an entrepreneur does is solving problems. They make something more efficient, provide a better service or build a new product that helps people in their everyday lives. Whatever it is that entrepreneurs are trying to sell, it's meant to change and improve lives (and turn a profit).

- You become a business leader

    Being able to see how your business has contributed to the local economy and provided jobs is incredibly rewarding. Your role as a business leader in your community is important and respectable.

- Excitement

    Part of what makes entrepreneurship so alluring is that it's both dynamic and exciting. The company is growing and adapting constantly, keeping everyone on their toes.

Some experience shared by entrepreneurs

- "When I quit and started my own business, I realized I could never go back to work for anyone else. I love being in control of my own destiny, choosing the clients I like to work with, and I even enjoy most of the challenges that business brings. I now work with small business owners, who are the backbone of the economy, and I love helping them to grow their businesses in turn." – Alastair McDermott, founder, WebsiteDoctor

- "I love being an entrepreneur because I am able to set my own schedule around my family life. Being a busy mom of two, I have the flexibility to schedule clients around my children's sports, school schedules and doctor appointments." – Stacy Haynes, CEO and counseling psychologist, Little Hands Family Services

- "Being an entrepreneur gives you the opportunity to take a calculated risk on a passion." – Francesco Clark, founder, Clark's Botanicals

- "Entrepreneurship constantly presents new challenges. As you overcome the adversity in your business, it leads to personal growth as well." – Marques Colston, director of new business, Main Squeeze Juice Co.

- "I love owning my own business because I feel there is always something that I can do to improve. Whether it be writing a new blog post, scheduling social media or reaching out to new organizations, there is always something to keep me busy." – Claire Coder, founder and CEO, Aunt Flow

- "Being an entrepreneur is awesome for a lot of reasons, but I think the most important and overlooked reason is that it forces a person to develop parts of their personality that make them more well-rounded and a better person." – Ian Ippolito, founder and CEO, Exhedra Solutions

- "Being an entrepreneur is great because you literally own your destiny. If you want to earn more money, work harder and it happens." – Natalie Bidnick Andreas, digital and content marketing strategist

- "The best part of being an entrepreneur is the ability to create something from nothing. I get to bring new programs and ideas to my clients and to hardworking professionals every day." – Kristi Daniels McNab, founder, Thrive 9 to 5

- "Nothing pushes me to work harder and smarter than the responsibility of having my name on the door. Running a business – and being responsible for other people's well-being and income – gives me the motivation and discipline to be the hardest-working version of myself." – Natalie Zfat, social media influencer and co-founder, The Social Co.

- "I think being an entrepreneur is great because the possibilities are endless. You can be as creative and innovative as you want to be, and the results are the most rewarding." – Anneliece Velasco, owner, Fred Astaire Dance Studio of Smithtown

- "Being an entrepreneur allows me to create my own definition of success. I do not have to sit at a desk for a specific period of time, turn in X number of projects and hit specific goals, or make it into the Presidents Club to be successful." – Danielle Tate, CEO, MissNowMrs.com

- "Being an entrepreneur is great because one can respond to opportunity quickly. In my previous corporate life, decision-making could take so long that the opportunity actually vanished before all the parties could get together to make a decision to proceed." – Peter Pierce, founder and CEO, Hamptons Salt Company

- "The best part of being an entrepreneur is contributing something larger than yourself. Entrepreneurs solve problems and bring a product or service to the world that people need. Sure, you have the opportunity to get paid well, but giving livelihood to others and crafting the world you want to see is way more fulfilling." – Matt Wilson, co-founder, Under30Experiences

- "My business is almost 100 percent online, so I also have the freedom to live in other countries as I work. It allows me to expand my mind, learn new languages and experience the world in a way few others do." – Jill Loeffler, owner, SFTourismTips.com

- "One of the things I enjoy the most about being a founder is creating a culture that supports my values." – Jessica Greenwalt, founder, Pixelkeet

- "At the end of the day, the best part of being an entrepreneur is that it forces me to become a better me. I am forced to learn, change, adapt, get tough and innovate, and since no one in the world could be harder on me than me, I will continue to improve." – William Kehler, founder, Manhattan Moonshine

- "Being an entrepreneur is greatest when it fulfills that inner desire to prove yourself right. It's the kind of satisfaction that only comes when you are growing at a remarkable pace and you have the gears in place to make it work right." – Cody Miles, creative director, Brandcave

- "Being an entrepreneur has allowed me to create a career that didn't even exist before I made it up." – Lisa Spector, co-founder, iCalmPet

- "Since starting my brand a few months ago, the best thing I must admit about being an entrepreneur is the social joy that I get to meet and converse with so many great, take-no-bullcrap, powerful women." – Crystal Etienne, founder and CEO, PantyProp

- "What I like best is that I feel like I'm actually doing something to make a difference. I'm really building something, really arranging a thing, rather than just pushing papers [and] digital files around for someone else." – Duke York, co-founder and director of finances, Punto Space

- "It's extremely rewarding to mentor and train new hires and then witness their development and growth to become leaders in the company." – Jordan Wan, founder and CEO, CloserIQ

- "For me, it is a source of energy [and] pride and leaves me at the end of each day knowing I worked incredibly hard and feeling fulfilled." – Ron Perry, founder, egniteBIZ

- "I can decide my own hours, and I can hire amazing people from all over to create the best team. I get to be the creator and see my business take shape and grow. What can be more exciting than that?" – Carina Tannenberg, owner, Bed of Nails

- "What I love most about having my own business is the ability to arrange my life around my own priorities, energy and preferred work rhythms." – Elene Cafasso, founder and president, Enerpace

- "As a social entrepreneur and designer, I am fueled by the conviction that entrepreneurship and design can be a vehicle for social change." – Colleen Clines, co-founder and CEO, Anchal Project

- "I view entrepreneurship as a laboratory and my business ideas as the ingredients. I have the freedom to use my ingredients as I wish as long as everything goes well!" – Neerav Mehta, co-founder and CEO, Red Crackle

- "I never feel like I'm going to work. It doesn't feel like work because I'm doing exactly what I want to do, and I enjoy it." – Darci Upham, franchise owner and vacation specialist, CruiseOne

- "To me, the best part is absorbing all the knowledge you can from every aspect of your business, getting mentors around you to help train you where you are lacking, and, last but not least, watching your ideas blossom and take off without extremely long chains of commands." – Chris Folayan, CEO, Mall for Africa

- "The entrepreneur community has a certain energy. Personally, I found it to be absent entirely from corporate America, and we thrive on it daily today." – Mike Solow, CEO and co-founder, Idea Harvest

- "We've all heard the story about the lion at the zoo and his cousin in the wild. I'd rather be running for my food and risk not eating than having slabs of meat thrown at me while I sit in a 12 x 12 concrete pit." – Kyle Eschenroeder, co-founder, StartupBros

- "Starting my own business has been empowering, challenging and exciting all rolled into one. Once I got through all the difficulties, I really grew into my own skin and it felt great! I love owning my own business and seeing how much I can grow both personally and professionally." – Whitney Carpenter, owner, Billwood Properties

- "I love being an entrepreneur because of control. Control has a negative connotation, but to me, it's something beautiful and powerful." – Felena Hanson, founder, Hera Hub

- "As an entrepreneur, you add value to society, as some product or service exists in the world because of you." – Mike Oeth, CEO, OnSIP

- "The greatest reason to be an entrepreneur? The incredible fairness of it – there's no force more fair in the world than the marketplace of ideas. The live-and-die fairness of the market awakens something inside of you – passion, hunger, fear – that makes you feel more alive than you've ever felt before." – David Yang, co-founder and lead instructor, Fullstack Academy

- "When my boss told me to stay in my lane, I knew I had to do something else. The day I walked into my office and had the ability to grow my company was the day I knew I was exactly where I was meant to be." – Brittany Ringersen, CEO and founder, Lighthouse Recovery Institute

- "The best part of being an entrepreneur is that you can get out of it exactly what you put in. The harder you work, the bigger the reward." – Elizabeth Henson, owner, Elizabeth Henson Photos

- "By far what I enjoy the most about being an entrepreneur is the ability to interact with a wide range of companies and individuals and to learn from them." – Linda Pophal, owner, Strategic Communications

- "I feel fulfilled when Fridays come along and I get to give my employees their paycheck. My business is a small business – fewer than 15 employees – so I know all my employees well and like talking to them about their work and mentoring them if/when they need it. Also, knowing that there are people that depend on me for their livelihood drives me to keep growing my business." – Priyanka Murthy, head designer and CEO, Arya Esha

- "As an employee, you are one ingredient in a recipe. You do not get to choose what gets cooked, how it is prepared or to whom it gets served. Additionally, your ingredient may be the one that will not make or break the recipe. As an entrepreneur, you have the freedom to design your own menu." – Karen Swim, owner, Words for Hire

- "To me, one of the best things about being an entrepreneur is you're helping shape the future of the world. Whether it's a new consumer product, B2B service or a new medical device, what you do can have a profound impact on the lives of others." – Tim Segraves, co-founder, Revaluate

- "I love that I get to decide who I help and how I help them. My clients are people I've chosen because I personally identify with them, so the problems I'm solving are both interesting and enjoyable. And I get to be creative in how I solve them, which would be harder to do as an employee." – Matt Becker, founder, Mom and Dad Money

- "The best part of being an entrepreneur is getting to meet so many talented entrepreneurs, changemakers and passionate people, whether online or in person. If I didn't have to push myself to make my business succeed, I would have never stepped outside of my introvert comfort zone and made the great connections I have now." – Dana Rivera, owner, Dana Rivera Films

3
Statistics of Entrepreneurship

At a high level, one fact is clear about the entrepreneurship trend: It's on an upward trajectory. After taking a steep decline during the U.S. recession between 2008 and 2011, it has rebounded and is now back to pre-recession growth rates.

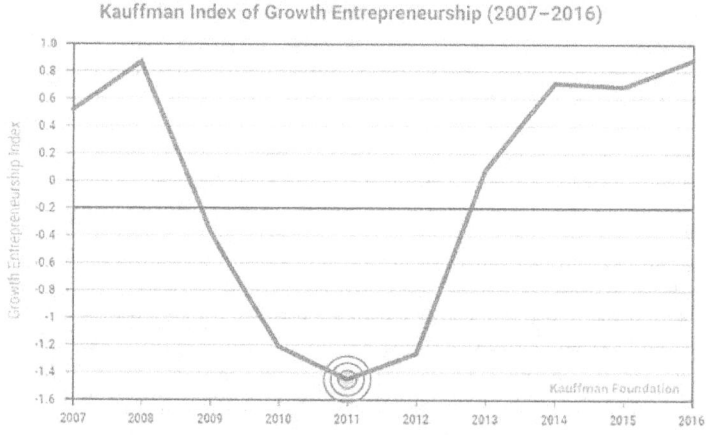

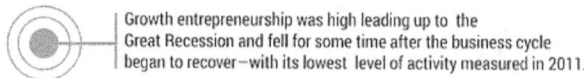

Growth entrepreneurship was high leading up to the Great Recession and fell for some time after the business cycle began to recover—with its lowest level of activity measured in 2011.

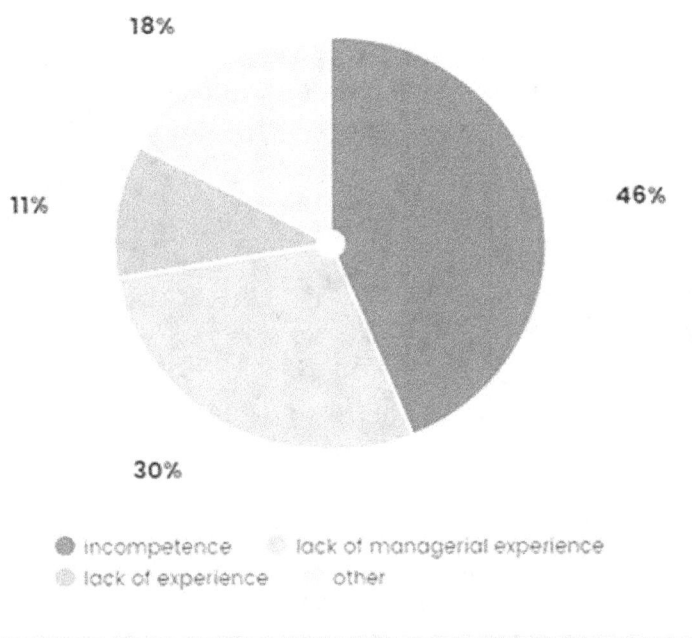

- incompetence
- lack of managerial experience
- lack of experience
- other

WHY DO PEOPLE BECOME ENTREPRENEURS?

Top 5 reasons why people start their own business

Money

Flexibility of being your own boss

Control over decision making

Pick the team you want to work with

Legacy: Leaving your footprint

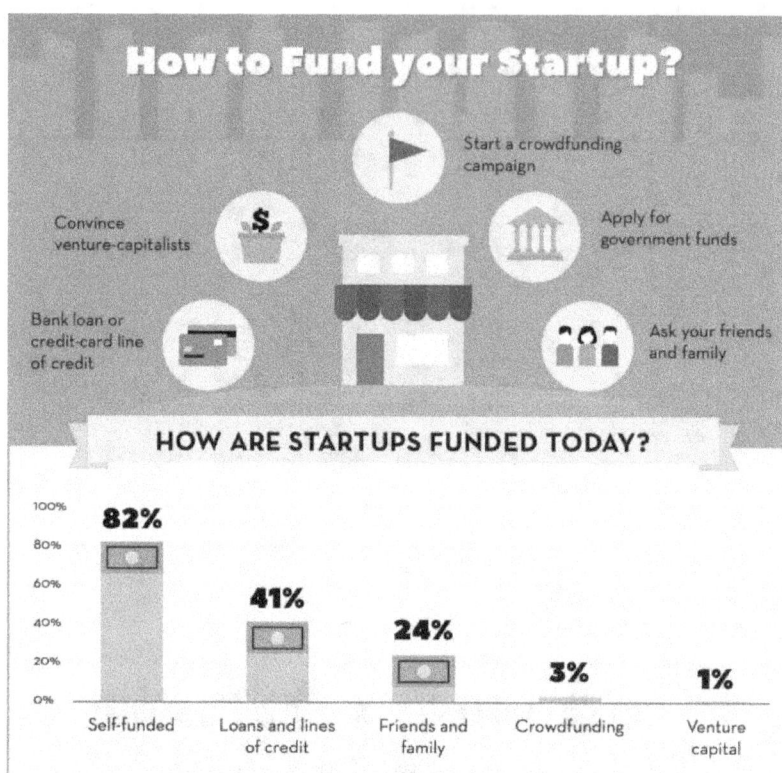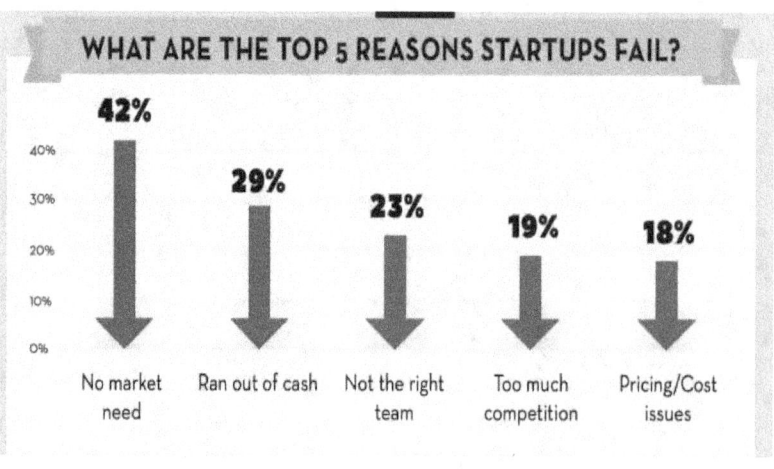

- **15 million Americans are self-employed full-time**

  This entrepreneurship statistic is likely to rise according to a 2018 FreshBooks report. It's estimated that 27 million Americans will leave **452,835 companies were founded in 2014, but this is less than 30 years ago.**

While one might assume the number of small businesses launched each year is increasing, it's been decreasing during the past few years due to reasons like industrialization, the Great Recession, and increased regulatory requirements.

- **Despite fewer businesses being started each year, business failure rates are on a long-term decline**
The rate at which American entrepreneurs closed shops has fallen by 30% since 1977.

- **There are various reasons why most businesses fail**
According to CB Insights, a surprising 42% of businesses fail because there is no market need. Around 29% fail because they ran out of cash, 23% don't have the right team to help them succeed, and 17% fail because they don't have a strong enough business model.

- **Roughly 80% of small businesses survive the first year**
The Small Business Administration (SBA) states that while nearly 80% of small businesses survive their first year, only 50% have survived five years or longer during the past decade. About one-third of small businesses survive 10 years or longer.

- **Entrepreneurs fund their business with their savings, profit, and business loans**
  About 21.9% of small firms have used personal and family savings to finance their business while 5.7% have used business profits and assets, and 8% have used business loans and credit cards from banks.

- **The average short-term business loan amount is $20,000**
  These are more accessible loans for smaller business endeavors. The average SBA loan amount is $417,316, and the average business line of credit is $22,000. Most small businesses are still applying for loans through traditional banks. The average loan amount from a traditional bank is around $150,000.

- **Most business owners start their own business from scratch**
  Approximately 83.1% founded their own business, 11.3% purchased, 2.8% inherited, and 4.4% transfer of ownership or gift.

- **Most small business owners don't have a college degree**
  A degree is not a requirement to start your own business. In fact, most business owners either never went to college or dropped out before they could obtain a degree. According to a CNBC/Survey Monkey

survey, only 26% of small business owners said they had a bachelor's degree. Only 17% went to college, 20% graduated high school but did not go to college, and 5% didn't graduate high school.

- **More than 50% of companies started in a garage or basement**
  If you're starting a business out of your home and not in an office, don't get discouraged. World-renowned companies like Google, Apple, Amazon, Microsoft, and Disney all started in a garage or basement. Currently, 51.6% of companies are started in someone's garage or basement.

- **More than 35% of entrepreneurs work 40 hours per week**
  This includes weekends as 17.7% say they work every weekend. About 31% of entrepreneurs work 50 hours per week and 11.8% work 60 hours per week. Working longer hours means that some business owners have to miss important lifestyle events, celebrations, and other experiences. About 37.9% say they missed a family or social occasion at least a few times per year due to work.

- **Entrepreneurs are 125% more successful if they've worked previous jobs in the industry they're currently doing business in**

While education may not be a huge factor, experience sure is when it comes to being a successful entrepreneur. Research shows that entrepreneurs are much more likely to be successful if they've held a previous job in the field their new business is in. This can be true for a variety of reasons, the most obvious one being experiences and connections. A more experienced candidate can charge more when they go into business for themselves, and they also have a better chance of providing more value to customer and clients.

- **62% of U.S. billionaires are self-made**
After surveying 585 billionaires in 2016, Wealth X determined that 362 or 62% were self-made, 18% reached billionaire status through a combination of inheritance and making their own wealth. The remaining 20% inherited their wealth.

UNITED STATE 6 MILLION NEW COMPANY INCORPORATE

70% SURVIVE 2 YEARS

50% SURVIVE 5 YEARS

25% LAST 15 YEARS

RISK NO REWARD

4

Why Entrepreneur Fail

Lack of Vision

It is an assumption that loving something or having so much passionate about a thing is enough reason to make it a business. But people don't understand the broader picture, the most necessary thing when starting a business is the vision. You have to realize that it is the starting point and where you would like to see yourself after 2, 5 or 10 years. A clear vision will help you to focus and can stop you from moving in a wrong direction.

Selection of a Business

Selection of business is eventually one of the top reasons why most entrepreneurs fail. One of the tricky moments in an entrepreneur's life comes when he or she decides which business to adapt. Yes, every business has a potential of millions in it, but you have to understand that not every business is appropriate for you. Doing proper research before selecting a business is essential. Write down pros and cons of every business idea that comes to your mind and then go with the most suitable one.

Lack of Proper Planning

Improper planning is another common reason why entrepreneurs fail and go out of the market. A lot of first-time entrepreneurs often neglect that having a business plan is a very vital part of starting a new business. The planning should include a long-term and a short-term strategy. Your business vision will help you to set a goal but to achieve that goal a master plan is a key.

Not Having Enough Capital

Starting a business without sufficient capital is almost certainly a suicide. New entrepreneurs often don't realize the importance of cash flow or underestimate the value of money they will need to run their startup smoothly. You may also take services of a financial advisory firm; they will help you to predict how much money you'll need to launch your business.

Poor Implementation of the Plan

A master plan is worth nothing without proper execution. There are many reasons behind the failure of implementation, but the most critical reason is ineffective leadership. Implementation of new strategies comes with enormous challenges; leaders must have the courage and determination to overcome them with patience.

The Hiring of Wrong People

Hiring the right people is vital to the success of any entrepreneur. Hiring a wrong person is not only a waste of resources, but it also creates a negative work environment which is not a good sign for your company. Instead of regretting a lousy hire, take a wise move to replace it with a right one.

Failure in Marketing

Marketing plays the vital role in the success of every business, and it is also among the most significant factors in the failure of entrepreneurs in 2018. You can get many potential buyers for the services or products you are offering with the marketing; it is a reliable process that can significantly contribute to your business success.

Expanding Very Early

The expansion and growth are the primary goals of every entrepreneur, but an early evolution can lead your business to death. You must decide about growth only after carefully reviewing and analyzing all the aspects. Just keep in mind, after the expansion it will be much harder to manage your business, and you must do it at an exact time.

Underestimating Competition

An important reason to mention for why entrepreneurs go out of business is underestimating the competition. To take a valuable share of a market, you must understand your competitors and think them as a severe threat. To increase your odds of success, keep a keen eye on your competitor's strengths and weaknesses.

Giving Up Very Early

The cause which is very common in the failure of every entrepreneur is that they give up and shut down all the projects. It's tough to encourage and pick you up in massive frustration, but there is no magic pill to turn failure into success. It's time to face the truth; the path of becoming a successful entrepreneur is full of hurdles and roadblocks. Instead of giving up, learn from your mistakes and try not to repeat them.

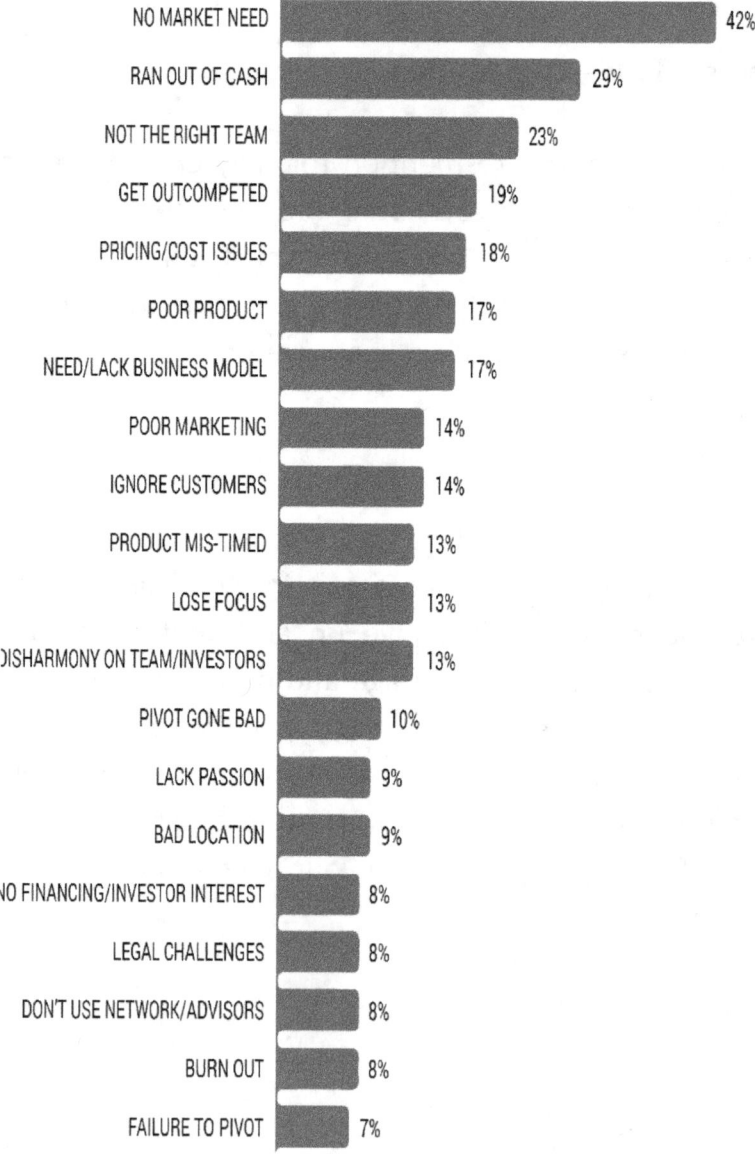

5

Lesson from an Entrepreneur

The most important life lesson entrepreneurs can teach you is that failure isn't necessarily bad. It shouldn't be the end to your entrepreneurial efforts. It shouldn't dissuade you from pursuing your other life goals either. In fact, failure should serve as a lesson and help you make better choices in the future.

Make calculated decisions

Impulsive behavior can be a huge setback for an entrepreneur. Regardless of the size of your business venture, you always have a lot at stake when making business decisions. So it's never a good idea to let your emotions control you. Instead, you need to make calculated decisions by weighing all the variables to ensure that there are no regrets.

Bill Gates set an excellent example of this when he claimed to have written a programming language for the MITS Altair 8000 even though he hadn't. He then worked with his childhood friend, Allen to develop what we now call BASIC.

Although he took a big risk, it was all calculated because he knew he could deliver.

Believe in yourself

As cliché as this may sound, entrepreneurs build success by learning to believe in themselves. Self-doubt can hold you back and prevent you from achieving your full potential. This holds true not just in the world of entrepreneurship but across all career fields.

If you don't believe in yourself, you're going to put too much importance on all the hurdles along the way. So you could find yourself holding back from executing an idea that has high chances of success just because of a negative feedback or a challenge. If Larry Page had listened to naysayers, we probably won't have Google today.

Learn to work with others

There is a very common misconception that successful entrepreneurs work alone and tend to be very controlling. But if you observe entrepreneurs like Sir Richard Branson closely, you'll find that the opposite is true. He maintains a healthy relationship with his employees and even writes personal letters to them.

That's why it's crucial that they learn to work well with others. Even if you consider yourself more of a loner, you need to find a way to adapt if you want to be successful. You should surround yourself with like-minded individuals who share the same passion of seeing your idea come to life.

It's not just about you or your competitors

According to Amazon's Jeff Bezos, entrepreneurs should obsess over their customers instead of obsessing over their competitors. Additionally, the needs of your customers should be more important than your own needs. By fulfilling your customers' needs, you can win their loyalty and eventually establish yourself as a successful entrepreneur, beating your competitors in the process.

Even in your personal life, learning to be selfless and to empathize with other people can get you a long way. A study published in PubMed Central even found that there's a striking correlation between selflessness and happiness.

Facing Fear of Failure

In life, it's a lot easier to just fly under the radar and keep your goals and achievements — and any failures to reach those goals — to yourself. Doing so helps you avoid a lot of embarrassment and judgment.
But when you start a business, you need to market it. You must put yourself out there in a very public way.
Something like 80-percent of businesses fail in the first year, so the odds are pretty stacked against you. And sadly, some

people actually are hoping to see you fail — including some of your peers.

Stay positive, ignore the naysayers, and learn from your mistakes so that things work out better the next time around. Some serial founders start multiple companies and look at each company as a learning experience, not a failure.

The 17 Mistakes Those Start-ups Make According To John Osher

Serial entrepreneur John Osher seems to have ambition in his vital organs. During the seven years he spent as a college undergraduate, Osher started and sold a vintage clothing store and an earring outlet. On the way to launching ConServ, his first major business venture, Osher worked as a cab driver, plumber and a carpenter. His second venture was Cap Toys, where sales volume reached $125 million. The company was sold to Hasbro, Inc. in 1997.

Osher has developed numerous consumer products, including an electric toothbrush that in just 15 months became America's best-seller in that category. As it turns out, his most valuable contribution to American business may not be the companies he's launched and profited handsomely from, but rather the startup advice that he's detailed and shared. When developing the plan for his third business, Dr. John's Products, Ltd., Osher sought to create and launch the perfect company and so he decided to make a list of everything he had done wrong as he built his previous two ventures.

In 1999, he used the list as a guide when he brought out Dr. John's SpinBrush, that previously mentioned electric toothbrush that retailed for $5.00. Maybe you bought one? The SpinBrush became wildly popular and in 2001, Proctor & Gamble bought him out for $475 million.

His list "17 Mistakes Start-ups Make" became a Harvard Business School case study in 2002. As you write the business plan that you'll use to launch and sustain your start-up venture, you will appreciate the practical advice provided by the inimitable John Osher.

1. **Failing to adequately research the concept to ensure it is viable**

"The most important mistake of all. I say nine out of ten businesses fail because the original concept is not viable. You want to be in business so much that you don't slow down and take the time to do the up-front research, so the business is doomed before the doors open. You can be very talented, but your business will fail because the concept is flawed."

Read magazines, journals, blogs and newsletters that cover the industry you plan to enter, so that you will fully understand the market you will enter and how to most advantageously position your product. Attend conferences when your budget allows and find free webinars. Confirm that you are about to enter an industry that is growing, not shrinking. Pay special attention to new developments or technology, the presence of major competitors and regulatory legislation that are on the horizon and poised to impact your ability to grow and sustain the business.

2. Miscalculating market size, timing, ease of entry and potential market share

"Most new entrepreneurs get very excited about their concept and don't look for the truth about how many people will want to buy what they they're selling."

Monitor and understand your market demographics, seasonal business cycles, potential barriers to entry and get to know how potential customers are getting their needs met now and what could motivate them to do business with you. Develop a credible business model.

3. Underestimating financial requirements and timing

"Based on inadequate research noted in Mistakes #1 & #2, fledgling entrepreneurs operate from the premise of over-stated market size and their ability to enter it. They then start spending more money than they should on start-up costs, creating costs that require those inflated sales projections to be met, so they run out of money."

4. **Over-projecting sales volume and timing**

"You have already miscalculated the size of the market. Now you over-project your portion of it."

5. **Under-projecting expenses**

"Cost projections are often far too low. Part of the problem is that you've projected market share and sales volume that are too high. There are always unknown reasons that come up to make expenses higher than planned."

6. **Over-spending on office space and equipment and employees**

"Now you've got lower sales, higher start-up costs and then you layer on too-high operating costs."

Resist the temptation to rent office space if you can operate effectively from a desk at home. If you can take clients to a restaurant for meetings and you otherwise work alone, then why increase your operating expenses? You can hire a telephone answering service to personally take messages, so it seems like you have an assistant. When you need another pair of hands to take on a big project, outsource tasks to a freelance Solopreneur and spread the wealth.

7. **Failing to have a contingency plan to cover a shortfall in sales**

"Even if you've been realistic about your ability to enter and penetrate your market, sales projections and start-up and operating expenses, there are things that happen when you start a new business. These aren't a result of poor planning, but they happen. Bank rates could go up. There could be a strike. You need a Plan B to cover yourself should things not work out within the timing that you want.

8. Bringing in the wrong or unnecessary partners

"There are certain partners you need. If you need money, you'll need money partners. But too many times the guy with the idea takes on his friends as partners. Many people don't provide strategic advantages. Before people are made partners, they have to earn it."

9. Hiring employees for convenience, rather than skill

"In my first business or two, I hired relatives but in many cases, they were wrong for the job. It's hard to fire relatives and friends. Spend time to handpick people based on skill requirements. It bogs you down when you hire people who can't do the job."

10. Neglecting to manage the entire company as a whole

"You see this happen all the time. They'll spend 50% of their time on something that represents 5% of the business. Too often, the business owner doesn't have a view of the whole company. They get involved in part, but don't manage the whole. Whether I handle this aspect or another, whether I hire someone to do what I can't, I consider how it all fits into the long-term and short-term big picture. Constantly try to see your big picture."

11. Accepting that "it's not possible" too easily, rather than finding a solution

"I had an engineer who was very good, but with every product we developed, he would say 'You can't do it that way.' I had to be careful not to accept this too easily. I had to look further. If you're going to be an entrepreneur, you're going to break new ground. A good entrepreneur is going to find a way.

12. Focusing on sales volume, rather than bottom-line profit

"Too much of your management is often based on sales volume and market size. There's too much emphasis on how fast and big you can grow the business, rather than on how much profit you can make."

13. Seeking confirmation of your actions, rather than seeking the truth

"This often happens: you want to do something, so you talk about it with people who work for you. You talk to family and friends. But you're only looking for confirmation. You're not looking for the truth. You're looking for somebody to tell you you're right. You have to learn to give more value to the truth than to people saying what you're doing is right."

14. Lacking simplicity in your business vision

"Rather than focusing on doing everything right to sell to your biggest markets, you divide your attention ...trying to be too many things at one time. Then your main product isn't done properly because you're doing so many different things."

15. Lacking clarity in the business purpose and goals

"You should have an idea of what your long-term aim is. It doesn't mean that it won't change, but when you aim an arrow, you aim it at a target. What are you trying to do? If you want to create a billion dollar company with a certain product, you may not have a chance. But if you're trying to create a million dollar company, then maybe with that product, you'll have a chance. Clarity of your business purpose is very important."

Have the confidence to embrace your long-term goals and do what is necessary to achieve them. What matters most is your vision for yourself and what you decide makes sense to pursue.

16. Lacking focus and identity

"This list was written from the viewpoint of building a company as a valuable entity. Remember that the company itself has an identity, a brand. Do not go after too many things at once and end up with a potpourri of products and services, rather than a focused business entity. When you go into business, it's important to maintain a focus and an identity. You must be focused on who you are and what you do and you build power and credibility from that."

This is a business model issue. Refrain from trying to touch as many target markets as possible, ready to use very skill set that you can muster. Being all things to all people results in an unfocused brand story and a diluted perception of your expertise. From your elevator pitch to your website and chosen social media platforms, potential clients must quickly understand how your products and services can help them. Sometimes, less is more.

17. Lacking an exit strategy

"Have an exit plan and create your business to satisfy that plan. You may build a business that you feel will start fast and make a good deal of money and for that reason will attract a lucrative buy-out. Maybe you figure that you can make lots of money for about two years but after that, competitors will enter and you won't be able to protect yourself from them. So after the first year, you watch the marketplace very carefully and keep a close eye on inventory. Another exit strategy can be to hand the company to your kids someday. The most important thing to do is build a company with value and profits so you have all the options open to you; keep the company, sell the company, go public, raise private money and so on. A business can be a product, too."

6

Mindset of an Entrepreneur

It is the Mindset that determines your thinking and your thinking determines the actions that you take. The actions you take unlock your true Greatness.

1. Clearly defines what it is that you want to do.

Very successful people care about their lives more than the average person. They take the time to analyze their lives, to look closely at their vision and their purpose in life. They put their lives on paper. They take the time to construct mental images that guide them on their journey. While most people are winging it, they put their life mission and business vision and goals on paper.

They have imagination. They pull their imagination up in their mind and then they define their vision and then they go to work. Night and Day!

2. Protect and Manage your Time.

Successful Entrepreneurs Protect and Manage their time. How many people do you know that plan their day before it begins?

The most valuable asset you have is your time. Plan your days, weeks, months, and years.

3. Outcomes Oriented

Have you known anyone that is absolutely driven to succeed? No matter what the obstacle they keep going. And in most cases it is because they have extraordinary clarity on the outcome.

They took the time to clearly define what it is that they wanted to do. They stopped and thought about their life, and what it was that they wanted to accomplish and this gave them the drive to see the task all the way to its outcome.

4. Deal with Actual Facts

Most people make their decisions about their life and careers from emotion and assumptions. Successful entrepreneurs base their decisions from fact-based thinking.

Successful entrepreneurs strive to make accurate decisions rooted in Actual Facts.

5. Live To Provide Value

Successful Entrepreneurs know that value must be given. And by providing value they know that value is to be returned.

They practice the Law of Reciprocity. They know for sure that what they give out they shall receive. Successful entrepreneurs do not expect something for nothing.

They are constantly working to make themselves valuable, which of course attracts the personal associations that lead to greater financial success.

6. Perform a Mind Makeover

Successful people rarely resemble the person that they once were. They are constantly educating themselves and gaining experience that will lead them to the goals they desire. They truly understand the importance of acquiring greater skill sets, which in turn gives them a confidence boost and greater self-worth.

They live by the words of 'renewing their minds'. These entrepreneurs know this is the key to their transformation and growth.

7. Focuses

This characteristic is what I have found to be the most important when it comes to entrepreneurial success.

Once you have awakened to the possibilities of success, you also realize the many opportunities that abound. And it is easy to allow yourself to become scattered.

Successful people develop the ability to focus and concentrate to maximize their resources and forces.

8. Successes by Association

Have you ever heard when growing up "be careful who you hang around'. Many times you may be 'guilty by association'.

Well, successful entrepreneurs understand that you can also be 'successful by association.'

In fact it is virtually impossible to be successful without having a mentor or a friend or business associate that helps to quicken your advancement.

Successful entrepreneurs have someone that accelerated their advancement with either some knowledge they possess or some other resource that they did not have.

9. Understand Self and Others

When you constantly work on yourself, you begin to develop a greater understanding of yourself and a greater belief in yourself, which translates into valuing yourself.

This is what allows you to become an expert in your chosen area. If you don't understand and value yourself you can bet the entire farm that no one else will understand or value you.

I have also found that those who understand and value themselves have a greater ability to understand and value others. This skill set is so important when you are seeking higher levels of success.

10. Take Personal Responsibilities

This trait is it. I mean this removes all attempts to blame anyone for what takes place in your life.

Successful entrepreneurs never allude to anything that anyone could have done to them. In fact, all the trials that they have, they looked at them as a blessing to learn from. Never giving up control of their lives.

I really love the fact of being in control of your life. Never allowing something outside to control you and the future of your family.

11. A Positive Mental Attitude

"When everything seems to be going against you, remember that the airplane takes off against the wind, not with it." – Henry Ford, founder of Ford Motor Company.

12. A Creative Mindset

"Creativity is just connecting things. When you ask creative people how they did something, they feel a little guilty because they didn't really do it, they just saw something. It seemed obvious to them after a while. That's because they were able to connect experiences they've had and synthesize new things." – Steve Jobs

13. Persuasive Communication Ability

"If you would persuade, you must appeal to interest rather than intellect."– Benjamin Franklin

14. Intrinsic Motivation and Drive

"The secret of change is to focus all your energy not on fighting the old but on building the new." – Socrates

15. Tenacity and an Ability to Learn from Failure

"Every failure is a step to success." – Malcolm Forbes

16. Gratitude

When you see life and career in terms of the lack in what you have achieved, you cannot drive your business up the ladder of success. Then negativity is impeding your progress.

You must look at all you have and realise how great what you have is as compared to the situation of many others.

When you have this attitude, you stop suffering and complaining about the small stuff. On each receipt you pay out, write thank you. That's not only to thank the person, event, vendor or customer for what's provided you but also to give a private thanks acknowledging that you have the abundance necessary to pay for the service, product or event.

7

Blueprint of Entrepreneurship

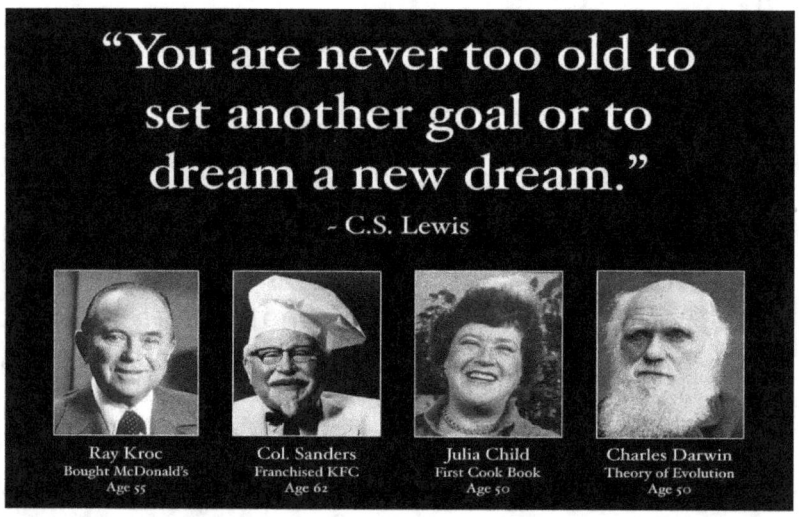

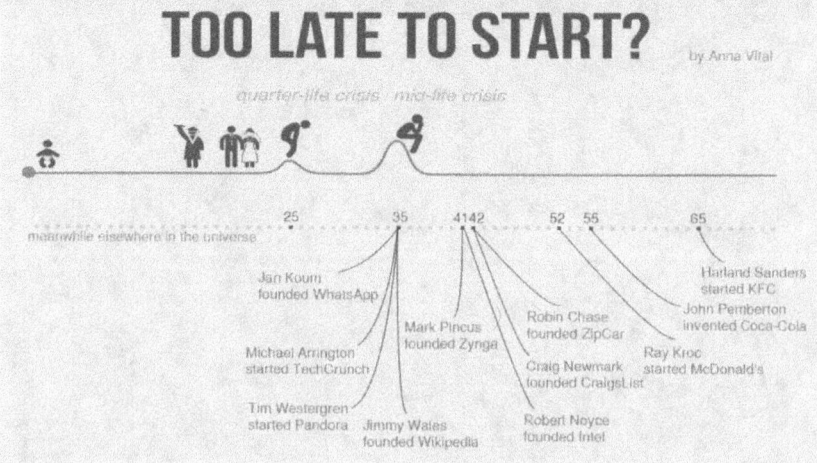

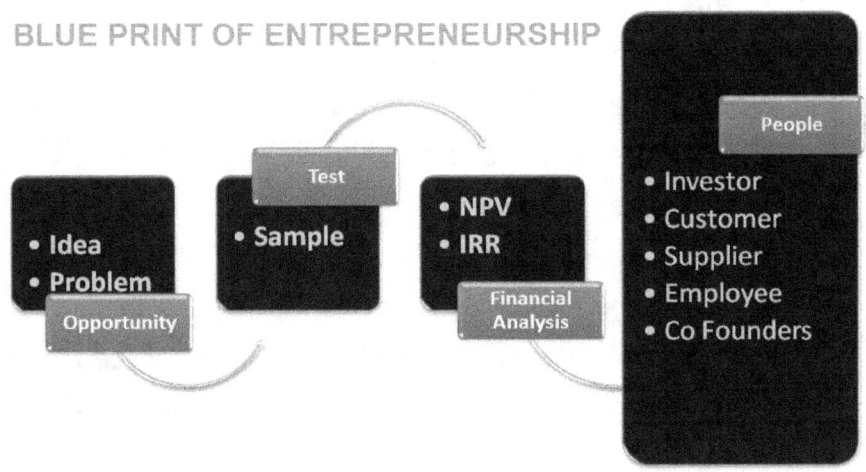

Q&A

- What Entrepreneurship mean to you in your life, what word come into your mind?
  Your Answer:-

- Who are the entrepreneurs you admire most?
  Your Answer:-
- Why do you admire them?
  Your Answer:-

- Who are your favourite company?
  Your Answer:-

- How they become so successful?
- Your Answer:-

In this blueprint, you will be learning:-
- What is entrepreneurship?
- How do they find opportunity and problem?
- How do they raise fund?
- How do they manage risk?
- How do they build team?
- How do they scale?
- What distinguishes the companies that succeed from those failed?

Blueprint is a tool for you to build up your own venture .what is the common characteristics of a successful venture? they have created and capture the customer value , customer are ready to pay more than the company capital cost , they have superior product compare with the competitions in the industry .They have a attractive business model to generate good cash flow , they have achieved economics of scale and network effects , they have great team in all hierarchy , they have barriers to entry and competitive advantage .Everybody can become entrepreneur all need a right product and a right team to build a successful company .

The entrepreneurship is a continuous process that needs to be followed by an entrepreneur to plan and launch the new ventures more efficiently.

Discovery: An entrepreneurial process begins with the idea generation, wherein the entrepreneur identifies and evaluates the business opportunities. The identification and the evaluation of opportunities is a difficult task; an entrepreneur seeks inputs from all the persons including employees, consumers, channel partners, technical people, etc. to reach to an optimum business opportunity. Once the opportunity has been decided upon, the next step is to evaluate it.

An entrepreneur can evaluate the efficiency of an opportunity by continuously asking certain questions to himself, such as, whether the opportunity is worth investing in, is it sufficiently attractive, are the proposed solutions feasible, is there any competitive advantage, what is the risk associated with it. Above all, an entrepreneur must analyze his personal skills and hobbies, whether these coincides with the entrepreneurial goals or not.

Developing a Business Plan: Once the opportunity is identified, an entrepreneur needs to create a comprehensive business plan. A business plan is critical to the success of any new venture since it acts as a benchmark and the evaluation criteria to see if the organization is moving towards its set goals.

An entrepreneur must dedicate his sufficient time towards its creation, the major components of a business plan are mission and vision statement, goals and objectives, capital requirement, a description of products and services, etc.

Resourcing: The third step in the entrepreneurial process is resourcing, wherein the entrepreneur identifies the sources from where the finance and the human resource can be arranged. Here, the entrepreneur finds the investors for its new venture and the personnel to carry out the business activities.

Managing the company: Once the funds are raised and the employees are hired, the next step is to initiate the business operations to achieve the set goals. First of all, an entrepreneur must decide the management structure or the hierarchy that is required to solve the operational problems when they arise.

Harvesting: The final step in the entrepreneurial process is harvesting wherein, an entrepreneur decides on the future prospects of the business, i.e. its growth and development. Here, the actual growth is compared against the planned growth and then the decision regarding the stability or the expansion of business operations is undertaken accordingly, by an entrepreneur.

We associate entrepreneurship with invention and innovation such as:-

Oprah Winfrey

I think Oprah Winfrey has one of the most amazing modern rags-to-riches stories of all time. As you're probably well aware, Oprah is the richest African American of the 21st century, and with a net worth of over $3 billion, she is regarded as arguably the most influential woman in the world.

Walt Disney

Walt Disney started off as a farm boy drawing cartoon pictures of his neighbor's horses for fun. When he was older, Walt tried to get a job as a newspaper cartoonist, but was unable to find one and ended up working in an art studio where he created ads for newspapers and magazines. Eventually he grew to work on commercials, became interested in animation, and eventually opened his own animation company.

J.K. Rowling

Today J.K. Rowling is a household name for fans of the beloved Harry Potter book series, but she wasn't always gifted with magic. The fact is, J.K Rowling was at her rope's end before her misfit gang of witches and wizards saved her. Before her bestseller cast a spell on readers, J.K. Rowling was living on welfare and struggling to get by as a single mother.

Steve Jobs

You can't really make a self-respecting "famous entrepreneurs" list without throwing in Steve Jobs. Jobs dropped out of college because his family couldn't handle the financial burden of his education. He unofficially continued to audit classes, living off free meals from the local Hare Krishna temple and returning Coke bottles for change just to get by. Jobs credited the calligraphy class he stopped in on as his inspiration for the Mac's revolutionary typefaces and font design.

Andrew Carnegie

Andrew Carnegie was born on November 25, 1835, in Dunfermline, Fife, Scotland. Although he had little formal education, Carnegie grew up in a family that believed in the importance of books and learning. The son of a handloom weaver, Carnegie grew up to become one of the wealthiest businessmen in America.

Carnegie had a really rough life growing up. He spent his childhood working in factories, and at night he forced himself to sleep as a way to forget his constant hunger.

John D. Rockefeller

Even though we give these Gilded Age guys a lot of tough love for being so filthy rich, you can't say they didn't do good with their fortunes.

One of the world's wealthiest individuals of all time, Rockefeller was born the son of a traveling salesman. He showed early entrepreneurial promise selling candy and doing odd jobs for neighbors, eventually going on to become the founder of the Standard Oil Company. There's no business quite like oil business, and it made Rockefeller filthy rich.

Bill Gates

Bill Gates is one of the most famous entrepreneurs of our era. The richest man in the world, Gates has a net worth estimated to be over $79 billion. He's held the title of "world's wealthiest individual" for 16 of the past 21 years.

Co-founder of the world's largest PC software company, Microsoft, Gates was one of the defining figures of the personal computer revolution.

Jeff Bezos

Jeffrey Preston Bezos is an American industrialist, media proprietor, and investor. He is best known as the founder, CEO, and president of the online retail company Amazon. The first billionaire on the Forbes wealth index, Bezos has been the world's richest person since 2017 and was named the "richest man in modern history" after his net worth increased to $150 billion in July 2018. In September 2018, Forbes described him as "far richer than anyone else on the planet" as he added $1.8 billion to his net worth when Amazon became the second company in history to reach a market cap of $1 trillion.

Warren Buffett

The famously humble Warren Buffett is an investor, businessman and philanthropist. Buffett is the CEO, chairman, and largest stockholder of the multinational holding company Berkshire Hathaway. He is also one of the wealthiest men in the world and has pledged to donate the bulk of his fortune to charity.

- *Describe yourself? What are your strengths and weaknesses?*
- *Your Answer:-*

BLUEPRINT OF ENTREPRENEURSHIP OPPORTUNITY
IDEA & PROBLEM

When you have made the leap to decide to start your own business the next step is determining which type of business you should start. Popular trends include businesses that help consumers save time and money.

A business idea is a concept that can be used for financial gain that is usually centered on a product or service that can be offered for money. An idea is the base of the pyramid when it comes to the business as a whole.

The characteristics of a promising business idea are:

- *Innovative*
- *Unique*
- *Problem solving*
- *Profitable*

For businesses, this could mean: creating new ideas, new product development through research and development, or improving existing services. Innovation can be the central focus of a business and this can help them to grow and become a market leader if they execute their ideas properly. Businesses that are focused on innovation are usually more efficient, cost-effective, and productive. Successful innovation should be built into the business strategy, where you can create a culture of innovation and drive forward creative problem-solving.

Examples of innovation

Apple was a $2 billion company in 1997, and then it jumped to a $700 billion valuation in 2015 as a result of the innovation that came from the Macbook, iPod, iPad, and iPhone.

Tesla built an electric car with exceptional aesthetics and efficiency, which has helped build the electric sports car company earn a market capitalization of $33 billion, with revenues up 54% since 2014.

Uber was founded in 2009 and has become a $50 billion company in just 6 years, with its simple yet unusual idea of getting a taxi with the press of a button that has completely revolutionized the way we book taxis.

These successful companies were built on sheer innovation and we can see how valuable they have become in the short time they have been around or have been focusing on innovation. When Tesla's value is compared to that of General Motors, we see that the market capitalization of General Motors is $53.98 billion today in which the company has been around since 1908 whereas Tesla was founded in 2003 and has achieved 50% of General Motors value within 12 years.

Q&A

- *Share your thought about the opportunity & Problem as an entrepreneur?*
- *Your Answer:-*

- *What opportunity you discover, that is still not discovered for the customer need and want?*
- *Your Answer:-*

- *Does customer will pay the price of the product or service you will offer?*
- *Your Answer:-*

- *Have you check the industry size, where you will enter?*
- *Your Answer:-*

- *Does the industry have barrier to entry and competitive advantage?*
- *Your Answer:-*

- *Does industry are growing, stable or shrinking?*
- *Your Answer:-*

- *Who will be your supplier?*
- *Your Answer:-*

- Who will be your competitors?
- Your Answer:-

- Which geographical area you will operate?
- Your Answer:-

- Who will be your team members?
- Your Answer:-

- You are in right direction or wrong, how you will evaluate?
- Your Answer:-

- The fund requires doing sampling of product or service?
- Your Answer:-

- What is your source of fund and in what terms?
- Your Answer:-

- What about other resources such as supplier, team members etc?
- Your Answer:-

- Once you done with product sampling, what you have learnt?
  Your Answer:-

- Customer like your product or service and what is your response?
Your Answer:-

- What are your further plans and any other product test?
Your Answer:-

FAILURE RATES OF STARTUPS

95% FALL SHORT OF MEETING PROJECTIONS

80% FAIL TO SEE PROJECTED RETURN ON INVESTMENT

40% LIQUIDATE AND LOSE MOST OR ALL INVESTMENT

99% OF REASON FOR FAILURE IS LACK OF PLANNING & EXPERIENCE

- What is your thought on venture fail?
- Your Answer:-
- 10%-20%
- 20%-40%
- 40%-80%
- 80%-100%

- *What you think the reason for venture fails?*
- *Your Answer:-*

- *If your venture fails, what will be your reflection?*
- *Your Answer:-*
- *Feel Depressed*
- *Lost money*
- *Lost someone else money*
- *Wrong decision*

How some of the great company have started, how they find the idea and opportunity and how they solve the problem of the people and become a great company such as facebook , starbucks , Alibaba ,Airbnb , Linkadins and Instagram .

Q&A

- *What is the opportunity you have discovered?*
- *Your Answer:-*

- *How you discovered the opportunity?*
- *Your Answer:-*

- *What piratical test you will execute to discover the opportunity is right?*
- *Your Answer:-*

- What you have learned from the test, what can go right and what can go wrong?
- Your Answer:-

- What you have learned from the test from many unresolved issues, ranging from pricing to selection to logistics. ?
- Your Answer:-

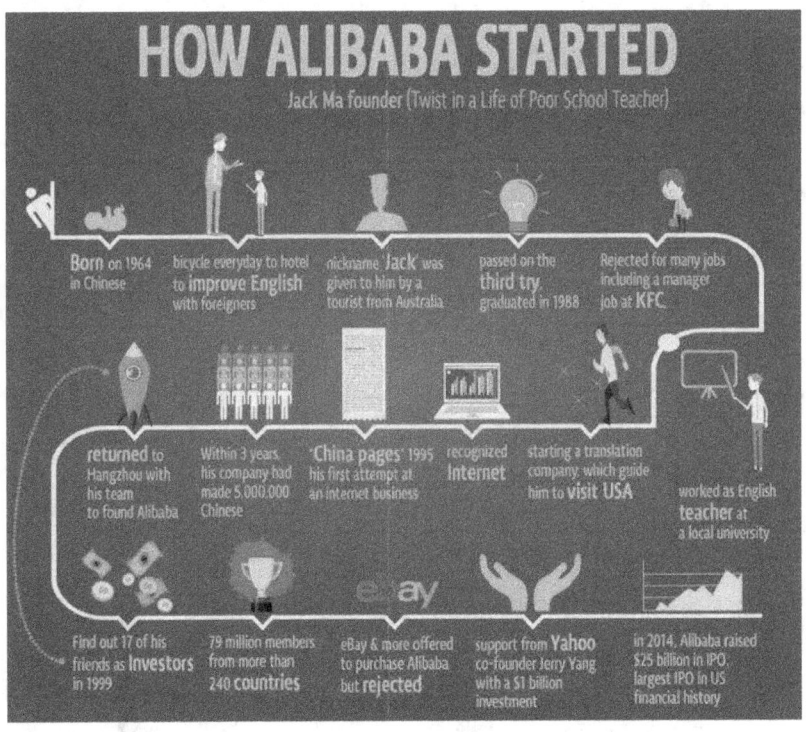

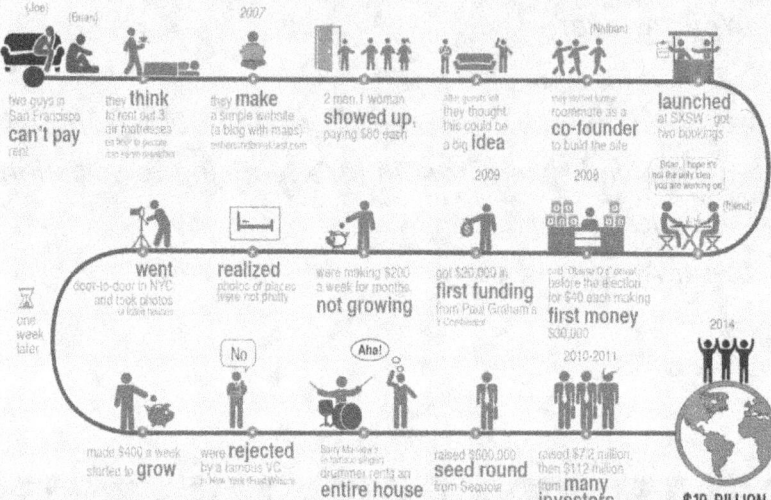
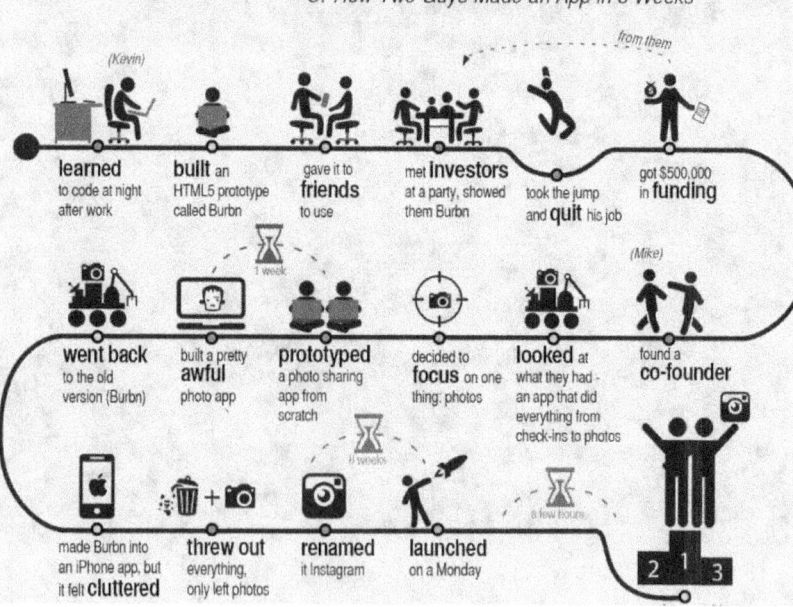

The Starbucks Story

Our story began in 1971. Back then we were a roaster and retailer of whole bean and ground coffee, tea and spices with a single store in Seattle's Pike Place Market. Today, we are privileged to connect with millions of customers every day in 76 markets.

Every day, we go to work hoping to do two things: share great coffee with our friends and help make the world a little better. It was true when the first Starbucks opened in 1971 and it's just as true today.

Back then, the company was a single store in Seattle's historic Pike Place Market. From just a narrow storefront, Starbucks offered some of the world's finest fresh-roasted whole bean coffees. The name, inspired by Moby Dick, evoked the romance of the high seas and the seafaring tradition of the early coffee traders.

In 1981, Howard Schultz (Starbucks chairman, president and chief executive officer) first walked into a Starbucks store. From his first cup of Sumatra, Howard was drawn into Starbucks and joined a year later.

The following year, in 1983, Howard travelled to Italy and became captivated with Italian coffee bars and the romance of the coffee experience. He had a vision to bring the Italian coffeehouse tradition back to the United States. A place for conversation and a sense of community. A third place between work and home. He left Starbucks for a short period of time to start his own Il Giornale coffeehouses and returned in August 1987 to purchase Starbucks with the help of local investors.

From the beginning, Starbucks set out to be a different kind of company. One that not only celebrated coffee and the rich tradition, but that also brought a feeling of connection.

Our mission: to inspire and nurture the human spirit – one person, one cup, and one neighbourhood at a time.

Today, with stores in more than 75 markets, Starbucks is the premier roaster and retailer of specialty coffee in the world. And with every cup, we strive to bring both our heritage and an exceptional experience to life.

The Airbnb Story

In 2007, designers Brian Chesky and Joe Gebbia couldn't afford the rent on their San Francisco apartment. To make ends meet, they decided to turn their loft into a lodging space, but, as Gebbia explains, "We didn't want to post on Craigslist because we felt it was too impersonal. Our entrepreneur instinct said 'build your own site.' So we did."

There was a design conference coming to town and hotel space was limited, so they set up a simple website with pictures of their loft-turned-lodging space—complete with three air mattresses on the floor and the promise of a home-cooked breakfast in the morning. This site got them their first three renters, each one paying $80, and after that first weekend they began receiving emails from people around the world asking when the site would be available for destinations like Buenos Aires, London, and Japan. Gebbia explains:

The following spring, they enlisted former roommate and engineer Nathan Blecharczyk to help them get Airbed & Breakfast off the ground. They planned the launch around the Democratic National Convention in order to capitalize on the resulting lack of hotel space. Fast forward seven years, and Airbed and Breakfast is now Airbnb—a household name that has surpassed industry legacy Hilton Hotels in nights booked. As of spring 2014, the platform had 10 million guests and 550,000 properties listed worldwide, along with a $10B valuation—making Airbnb worth more than legacy players like Wyndham and Hyatt. The company has received $776.4M from investors like Y Combinator, Sequoia Capital, Keith Rabois, Andreessen Horowitz, Ashton Kutcher, Founders Fund, and TPG Growth in a total of seven funding rounds—the last of which raised $500M alone.

Some of the example of the company that create value to the customer such as:-

- Uber is a platform where those who drive and deliver can connect with riders, eaters, and restaurants. In cities where Uber is available, you can use the Uber app to request a ride. When a nearby driver accepts your request, the app displays an estimated time of arrival for the driver heading to your pickup location.

- Facebook is a website which allows users, who sign-up for free profiles, to connect with friends, work colleagues or people they don't know, online. It allows users to share pictures, music, videos, and articles, as well as their own thoughts and opinions with however many people they like.

- Alibaba is China's and by some measures, the world's biggest online commerce company. Its three main sites Taobao, Tmall and Alibaba.com have hundreds of millions of users, and host millions of merchants and businesses.

- Airbnb is an online marketplace which lets people rent out their properties or spare rooms to guests. ... There are photos of the property, and the hosts/guests, with full map listing.

Questions to find opportunity

Q&A

- *The new model working in other country, will it work in my country?*
- *Your Answer:-*

- Can I apply new technology?
- Your Answer:-

- Can I reduce the cost of the product or Services?
- Your Answer:-

- Can I use current product and services in new business model?
- Your Answer:-

- Can I find out what their main problems are the best solutions for those problems, and the ideal ways to present the solutions to them?
- Your Answer:-

- How big is our potential market?
- Your Answer:-

- Will this market grow or shrink in the future?
- Your Answer:-

- What other products and services are similar to ours?
- Your Answer:-

- Who are our top competitors?
- Your Answer:-

- What market share do our competitors own?
- Your Answer:-

- What share is available for us to own/take?
- Your Answer:-

- How much inventory will be required?
- Your Answer:-

- Can customer become the repeat users?
- Your Answer:-

- How much cost for marketing to acquire customer?
- Your Answer:-

- What technology platform venture can use?
- Your Answer:-

- How much fund require starting the venture?
- Your Answer:-

- How much fund require for each stage of scale up the venture?
- Your Answer:-

- What is the time frame require for start the business operation?

Calculate total market size for a venture

Firms are always concerned with the size of the potential market for their products or services and the proportion of that market they actually reach—often referred to as a company's market share. Market share is the percentage of the total market (or industry) sales made by one firm. As a formula, Market Share = Firm's Sales ÷ Total Market Sales. Share can be reflected as either percentage of sales dollars, percentage of units sold, or percentage of customers. Percentage of sales dollars is the most common reference.

Market share is one of the most commonly quoted measures of success in any industry. To correctly determine market share, one must clearly define the market. Having a small share of a large market can be as profitable as a large share of a small market. A producer of leather horse saddles must determine if his market is made up of saddle sales, equestrian sales, or all leather goods sales. Obviously, his market share in the saddle industry is much larger than his share in the leather goods market.

There are two sources for measuring market share: competitors and consumers. Surveying competitors gives a more accurate and reliable picture of market share. It is possible to interview 100 percent of competitors, but not all consumers. To get a reliable figure from consumers, a large number of people would have to be interviewed. For many industries, sales and market share figures may already be compiled by government agencies, trade associations, or private research firms.

One of the most important determinants of a new venture's success is calculating the total potential market size and value. Knowing this figure helps determine how much money your business can make and also competitive market share. Whether you're creating a business around a new product or service, or coming out with a different version of something that already exists, it's important to determine the overall size of your market. This information will be highly valuable as you reach out to potential investors for funding and banks for loans. Additionally, you should always be aware of how many customers you could potentially serve.

What does market size mean? Basically, it's the number of customers potentially interested in your product or service, and the total possible amount of money that could be spent on that product or service. It sounds easy enough, but how do you measure something intangible?

This guide breaks down the five steps to estimating your market size providing specifics on where to find the information. The following are key steps in calculating both the market size in quantity of people, and market value:

Market Share Formula

$$\text{Market Share} = \frac{\text{Total Sales of the Company}}{\text{Total Sales of the Market}} \times 100$$

$$\text{Market Share} = \frac{\text{Total Number of Units Sold by the Company}}{\text{Total Number of Units Sold in the Market}} \times 100$$

1. Define the total geographical population.

2. Define the market segment and estimate the percentage of target customers in that area.

3. Estimate average number of items purchased at a time.

4. Estimate average purchase frequency.

5. Calculate selling price.

The following formula is used to estimate the total size of your product or service's market. Keep in mind that this is not necessarily how much your company can capture, but the total amount possible in the market. The market size is calculated by determining a value for all of the variables and then multiplying them together.

MS = TC * Q * F * P

MS = Market Size

N = Total Geographical Population

TC = Percentage of Target Customers in Geographical Area

Q = Quantity purchased at a time

F = Purchase Frequency in a year

P = Price of Product

This formula is simple but powerful, providing a holistic view of the market you are entering, including the potential revenues, and sales volume. As a beginning entrepreneur, it can sometimes be difficult to estimate values for each of the variables.

To calculate your market size, you'll either be looking for data on the number of potential customer, or number of transactions each year.

For example; if you are selling toothbrushes, virtually everyone can be counted in your big whole market figure. If people are listening to their dentists, and they are purchasing new toothbrushes 2-4 times per year, that number is even larger. If you are selling houses, then there may only be an average of 5.34M transactions in a good year, in the entire United States.

If your company makes a great new kind of ice cream bar that is exceptionally popular in your test markets, you might say that your market size is based on the $10 billion annual ice cream sales data. But that assertion would be inaccurate, because ice cream novelties (individually wrapped ice cream bars and popsicles) represent only 20 percent of the total ice cream market.

More accurately, you could say that your market size is $2 billion per year. You might even reduce that further by acknowledging that you'll distribute only regionally, as is the trend in the ice cream market. With those parameters in mind, your addressable market is reduced to $500 million per year.

If your strategy is to pursue the market through grocery and convenience store sales, your final numbers would need to take into account that the take-home market for ice cream is 67 percent of the market, making your addressable market only $335 million — a long way from your initial claim of $10 billion!

Create Competitive Advantage for Venture

Competitive advantage refers to factors that allow a company to produce goods or services better or more cheaply than its rivals. These factors allow the productive entity to generate more sales or superior margins compared to its market rivals.

Competitive advantages are attributed to a variety of factors including cost structure, branding, and the quality of product offerings, the distribution network, intellectual property, and customer service.

A firm's ability to produce a good or service more efficiently than its competitors, which leads to greater profit margins, creates a comparative advantage. Rational consumers will choose the cheaper of any two perfect substitutes offered. For example, a car owner will buy gasoline from a gas station that is 5 cents cheaper than other stations in the area. For imperfect substitutes, like Pepsi versus Coke, higher margins for the lowest-cost producers can eventually bring superior returns.

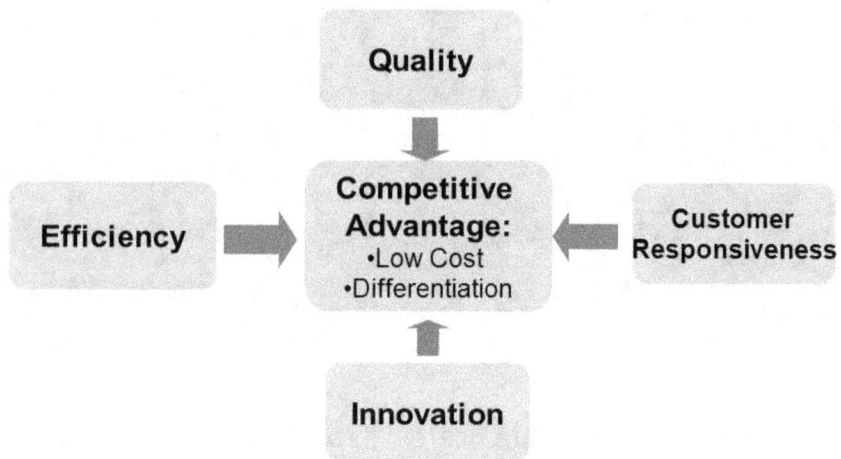

Economies of scale, efficient internal systems, and geographic location can also create a comparative advantage. Comparative advantage does not imply a better product or service, though. It only shows the firm can offer a product or service of the same value at a lower price.

For example, a firm that manufactures a product in China may have lower labor costs than a company that manufactures in the U.S., so it can offer an equal product at a lower price. In the context of international trade economics, opportunity cost determines comparative advantages.

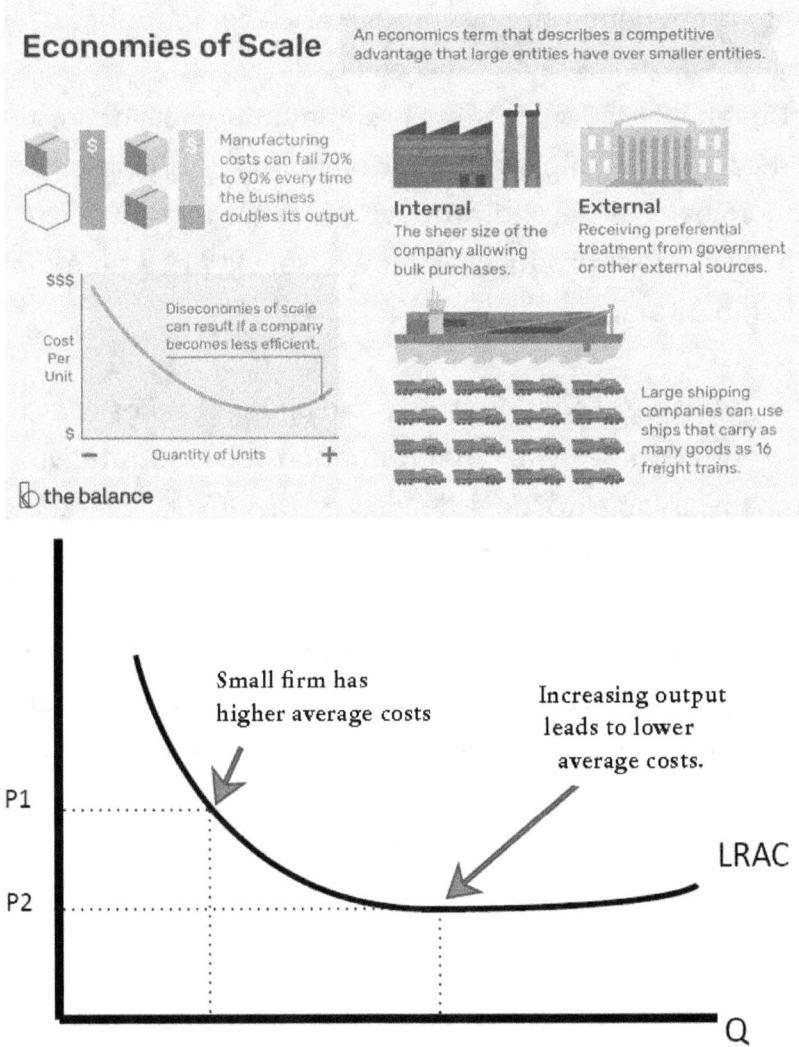

Amazon (AMZN) is an example of a company focused on building and maintaining a comparative advantage. The ecommerce platform has a level of scale and efficiency that is difficult for retail competitors to replicate, allowing it to rise to prominence largely through price competition.

McDonald's: McDonald's main competitive advantage relies on a cost leadership strategy. The company is able to utilize economies of scale and produce products at a low cost and as a result, offer products at a lower selling price than that of its competitors.

Louis Vuitton: Louis Vuitton's advantage relies on both differentiation and a differentiation-focus strategy. The company is able to be a leader in the luxury market and command premium prices through product uniqueness.

Walmart: Walmart's advantage relies on a cost leadership strategy. Walmart is able to offer 'everyday low prices' through economies of scale.

Create Economic Moat for Venture

The term economic moat, popularized by Warren Buffett, refers to a business' ability to maintain competitive advantages over its competitors in order to protect its long-term profits and market share from competing firms. Just like a medieval castle, the moat serves to protect those inside the fortress and their riches from outsiders.

Remember that a competitive advantage is essentially any factor that allows a company to provide a good or service that is similar to those offered by its competitors and, at the same time, outperform those competitors in profits. A good example of a competitive advantage would be a low-cost advantage, such as cheap access to raw materials. Very successful investors such as Buffett have been adept at finding companies with solid economic moats but relatively low share prices.

One of the basic tenets of modern economics, however, is that, given time, competition will erode any competitive advantages enjoyed by a firm. This effect occurs because once a firm establishes competitive advantages, its superior operations generate boosted profits for itself, thus providing a strong incentive for competing firms to duplicate the methods of the leading firm or find even better operating methods.

There are several ways in which a company creates an economic moat that allows it to have a significant advantage over its competitors. Below, we will explore some different ways in which moats are created.

Cost Advantage

A cost advantage that competitors cannot replicate can be a very effective economic moat. Companies with significant cost advantages can undercut the prices of any competitor that attempts to move into their industry, either forcing the competitor to leave the industry or at least impeding its growth. Companies with sustainable cost advantages can maintain a very large market share of their industry by squeezing out any new competitors who try to move in.

Size Advantage

Being big can sometimes, in itself, create an economic moat for a company. At a certain size, a firm achieves economies of scale. This is when more units of a good or service can be produced on a larger scale with lower input costs. This reduces overhead costs in areas such as financing, advertising, production, etc. Large companies that compete in a given industry tend to dominate the core market share of that industry, while smaller players are forced to either leave the industry or occupy smaller "niche" roles.

High Switching Costs

Being the big fish in the pond has other advantages. When a company is able to establish itself in an industry, suppliers and customers can be subject to high switching costs should they choose to do business with a new competitor. Competitors have a very difficult time taking market share away from the industry leader because of these cumbersome switching costs.

Intangibles

Another type of economic moat can be created through a firm's intangible assets, which includes items such as patents, brand recognition, government licenses and others. Strong brand name recognition allows these types of companies to charge a premium for their products over other competitors' goods, which boosts profits.

Sources of Economic Moats

- Network Effect

- Cost Advantage

- Intangible Assets

- Switching Costs

- New! Efficient Scale

Market Realist

Source: Morningstar

Q&A

- *Does your product or service have competitive advantage?*
- Your Answer:-

- *Does your product or service have economic moat?*
- Your Answer:-

- *What kind of team, you will form for your venture and how would you find them?*
- Your Answer:-

- *Have to check the industry size?*
- Your Answer:-

- What market share your venture will capture from the industry size?
- Your Answer:-

- Who is your customer and what is customer base?
- Your Answer:-

- Does customer willing to pay to your product or service?
- Your Answer:-

- Does your product or service have real and perceived value to the customer?
- Your Answer:-

- Have you made your business model and how venture make money?
- Your Answer:-

The End Point of Venture

When is an entrepreneurial journey complete? Sometimes, there's no clear endpoint. Companies may form and continue to grow. In other cases, the company fails, which signals a clear end to that particular journey. But now let's talk about one type of endpoint: selling a company.

What do you think is the best possible exit plan for venture and Why?

An exit strategy is a contingency plan that is executed by an investor, trader, venture capitalist, or business owner to liquidate a position in a financial asset or dispose of tangible business assets once predetermined criteria for either has been met or exceeded.

An exit strategy may be executed to exit a non-performing investment or close an unprofitable business. In this case, the purpose of the exit strategy is to limit losses.

An exit strategy may also be executed when an investment or business venture has met its profit objective. For instance, an angel investor in a startup company may plan an exit strategy through an initial public offering (IPO).

An effective exit strategy should be planned for every positive and negative contingency regardless of the type of investment, trade, or business venture. This planning should be an integral part of determining the risk associated with the investment, trade, or business venture.

A business exit strategy is an entrepreneur's strategic plan to sell their ownership in a company to investors or another company. An exit strategy gives a business owner a way to reduce or liquidate their stake in a business and, if the business is successful, make a substantial profit.

If the business is not successful, an exit strategy (or "exit plan") enables the entrepreneur to limit losses. An exit strategy may also be used by an investor such as a venture capitalist to prepare for a cash-out of an investment.

For traders and investors, exit strategies and other money management techniques can greatly enhance their trading by eliminating emotion and reducing risk. Before entering a trade, an investor is advised to set a point at which they will sell for a loss and a point at which they will sell for a gain.

Money management is one of the most important (and least understood) aspects of trading. Many traders, for instance, enter a trade without an exit strategy and are often more likely to take premature profits or, worse, run losses. Traders should understand the exits that are available to them and create an exit strategy that will minimize losses and lock in profits.

If you continue losing money after having tried a variety of approaches to stabilize the business, it may sometimes be best to call it quits. Quitting might be a wise decision if you are several years into your venture and still have no traction; customers still respond to your sales pitch with a blank stare.

You can read some informative anecdotes about failing businesses here. Continued operations may result in additional losses which will further erode your net worth.

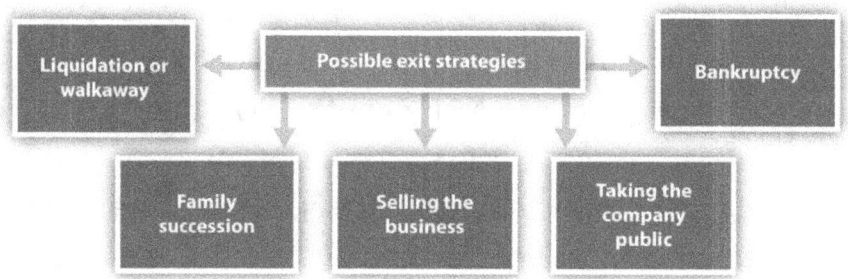

RIGHT PEOPLE

Selecting right people for your venture is one of the very vital area , is the people capable enough to be in team , is the right people to do the testing of the product or services ?so the people know that industry . The first step is to assemble people who are willing and able to work together as a team.

Most new entrepreneurs work alone in developing their idea or a solution to a problem, but ultimately realize that starting and growing a business requires more.

Not many people have the bandwidth to simultaneously cover all the required bases in finance, marketing, manufacturing, and operations, as well as solution development. It takes a working team to build a business.

What many don't realize is that building that team is as critical and as difficult as building the solution. If you have the wrong people on your team, or the team can't work together, you have no chance of making an epic business, no matter how great your solution.

Witness the many memorable failure examples, including Friendster, Pets.com, and Webvan.

Define your desired business culture and find people who fit.
The first step is to assemble people who are willing and able to work together as a team. Getting subject matter experts is necessary but not sufficient.

Finding interns or family members to save money won't work. You need team members who are aligned in their thinking and action.

Make sure the team embodies a common definition of success.
Find people who share your vision of success and have confidence in you and what you are setting out to do. Teams that do big things do not team casually or randomly.

They are willing and able to leverage failure, without losing confidence, since every business has many unknowns.

Everyone must choose to contribute, activate, and connect.

Each team member must be determined to bring their best to the role, bring out the best in others, and choose to partner across their areas of expertise to deliver on the shared objective of a successful new business.

Make it clear how you will measure each person's results.

Foster solid relationships to keep focus on what matters.

It's impossible for a team to effectively focus its energy on executing a plan when team members are distracted by poor relationships with one another.

If you want epic team results, equip team members to have epic relationships, and clearly communicate purpose and milestones expected.

Energize the team around a shared purpose and reality.

A team can only build a successful business when the members of that team have an open mind that is receptive to your vision of changing the world.

Energy that is being used to protect you cannot simultaneously be used to build the connections necessary for the team to succeed.

An advisory board is an informal group of local business professionals who can help you run your business better. And because advisory boards are unofficial (i.e., it's not the same as a corporate board of directors), you have a great deal of latitude in how you set it up. Advisory boards can be structured both to help with the direct operation of your company and to keep you informed on various business, legal and financial trends that may affect you and your business

Generally, you'll want a legal advisor, an accountant, a marketing expert, a human resources expert and perhaps a financial advisor. You may also want successful entrepreneurs from other industries who understand the basics of business and will view your operation with a fresh eye. If you don't personally know people with those areas of expertise, don't be afraid to ask the most successful people you can find. At best, you'll partake of the knowledge your community's successful business leaders have.

Advisory board members are rarely compensated with more than an occasional meal. Keep in mind that, instead, your advisory board members will likely benefit in a variety of tangible and intangible ways. Being on your board will expose them to ideas and perspectives they may have otherwise missed. It will also expand their own networks, which can offer a wide range of advantages.

When holding actual meetings, you can go one of two ways: You can either bring everyone together every month or two, or you can meet with different advisors separately in a way that makes sense to the issue at hand. It really depends on your business's needs, what you're comfortable with and the dynamic you wish to develop between your advisors.

How to Put a Board of Advisors Together

Creating a Board of Advisors is a task simpler said than done .However, there are tips to remember that will help business owners put together the kind of board that will bring the company to fruition.

#1 Identify who needs to be part of the board
Members of the Board of Advisors shouldn't just be those the owners are familiar with. They have to be screened against a certain set of standards such as having relevant experience in the industry where the business operates.

#2 creates a board of no more than five advisors
The ideal number should be between three and five. Putting more than five together can turn simple brainstorming sessions into complicated ones, reducing the overall productivity of the board.

#3 Does not include people who will only be making a living out of being a member of the Board of Advisors Ideally.

The members of the board should be working a separate full-time job, but they should also be interested in growing the business. They should also not be immediate family members or relatives whose emotional connection to the business may interfere.

	Manpower	
1	Experience	what they have done in there life
2	Track Record	what have they accomplished
3	Skills	what they know and how to do
4	Network	who knows them and whom they know
5	Attitude	what drives them
6	Character	how do they behave

The costs of a bad hire add up quickly--including training and salary costs, as well as costs associated with other employees picking up a bad employee's slack. According to data from the U.S. Department of Labor, the costs of a bad hire can add up to 30 percent of the hire's annual salary.

In some cases, you might keep a bad hire on board to stay fully staffed--only to finally hire someone when it's gotten out of hand. Doing so can have a negative impact on your team's productivity and profitability.

If you notice your team has made several bad hires in recent memory, it's likely time to rethink your hiring process. Many businesses make the mistake of hiring employees too quickly to fill open roles. Hiring the right employee is much more important than simply filling a seat.

Check in with your employees following a bad hire. Individual team members often end up getting overworked due to a bad hire that isn't performing, or even mistreated by a bad hire that isn't a culture fit for your team.

Q&A

- *Think about entrepreneurial ventures you are familiar with. What was the founding team like? Were they friends, industry experts, or some other category? Did the founding team stay with the company for a long time? Why or why not?*
- *Your Answer :*

- *Who is on your team? What qualities, characteristics, and skills do they have? How did you find these people?*
- *Your Answer :*

- *The fund you have arranged from people is right amount or too little?*
- *Your Answer :*

- The fund you have arranged from people at what team and conditions?
- Your Answer :

- The funds you have arranged from what kind of people are they such as family, friends, venture capital or bank?
- Your Answer :

- What qualities would you look for in potential employees?
- Your Answer :

- What do you think is more important: attitude or experience? Or both?
- Your Answer :

- According to data from the U.S. Department of Labor, the costs of a bad hire can add up to 30 percent of the hire's annual salary. What are the most common hiring mistakes?
- Your Answer :

- How do you think about building a team for your venture? What kind of team would you yourself like to join?
- Your Answer :

- You want people to join who want to make next Amazon or the people who want to join Amazon?
- Your Answer :

FINANCIAL ANALYSIS

An investor is any person or other, who commits capital with the expectation of receiving financial returns. Investors rely on different financial instruments to earn a rate of return and accomplish important financial objectives while investing in a venture.

The first type of investor entrepreneurs should be approaching at the very beginning is friends and family and close personal contacts.

These aren't true investors like the others on this list, but they can be sources of capital. Traditional banks are generally not an easy source of capital for early stage start-ups and small businesses. However, as you gain traction they may offer business credit cards, lines of credit and merchant advance loans.

Professional angel investors are normally approached when it comes to the seed round and beyond. They are willing to fund smaller operations than VCs, may be more flexible in terms, and can offer a lot of value in wisdom and connections.

Venture capital is a form of private equity and a type of financing that investors provide to startup companies and small businesses that are believed to have long-term growth potential. Venture capital generally comes from well-off investors, investment banks and any other financial institutions. However, it does not always take a monetary form; it can also be provided in the form of technical or managerial expertise. Venture capital is typically allocated to small companies with exceptional growth potential.

Causes of Co-founders Fall Out

Not having the same business goals

Selecting the wrong partner and/or getting the wrong fit, is often the key problem behind co-founders fall out.

No startup has an easy ride and the bumpy ride that is almost guaranteed will put that co-founding team under enormous pressure.

Not investing resources equally

In order to prevent resentment and tension build up, it is important that co-founders try to invest equally in their time, resources and wider assets.

If not investing resources equally, there will clearly need to be a conversation about how the equity is divided, to be confirmed within the agreement. The agreement will map out whether equity in the company is going to be shared equally among the co-founders or if there needs to be an agreement based on the percentage of resources that co-founders contributed.

Not having a great fit

As mentioned above, a crucial element in achieving a well-functioning relationship is that co-founders complement and support each of your mutual strengths and weaknesses. This perspective can take many different forms.

Understanding what those strengths and weaknesses are is an initial and crucial step to forming a strong team, and where you need to be most supportive or conversely, know when to step away.

Lack of communication

Honesty (or lack of) is also a key problem when it comes to communication and, failure to communicate within a hard pressed startup can be fatal.

Honest communication channels are such an important factor in a successful co-founder relationship.

Avoiding Conflict

It is understandable that once your startup is starting to gain traction, that you and your co-founders want to avoid conflict at all costs, often in fear that this will then cause more conflict.

This is counter-productive, as problems brushed under the carpet will often lead to even bigger emerging later down the track.

Case Study

Monetary value of a Venture

Investment	$1 Million
Units Sold	10,00,000
Retail Unit Price	$20
Retailer Margin	$5
Price to Product	$15
Manufacturer Price	$10
Selling Unit Cost	$3
Retail Sales	$150,00,000

Financial Model

Year	0	1	2	3
Revenues		$150,00,000	$150,00,000	$150,00,000
Cost of Goods Sold		$100,00,000	$100,00,000	$100,00,000
Gross Margin		$50,00,000	$50,00,000	$50,00,000
Selling Expense		$30,00,000	$30,00,000	$30,00,000
Operating Profit		$20,00,000	$20,00,000	$20,00,000
Taxes @ 25%		$5,00,000	$5,00,000	$5,00,000
Net Income		$15,00,000	$15,00,000	$15,00,000
Net Cash Flows	($10,00,000)	$15,00,000	$15,00,000	$15,00,000

You need one to build an economically viable business. Why? Because by quantifying (and then validating) your business plan and business model, assumptions and vision you are able of finding out whether you can turn your ideas into a sustainably operating business.

Moreover, if you build different versions ("scenarios") you are better prepared for the future, especially if things do not go the way you planned. What if you launch half a year later? Answering such a question in your "worst case scenario" helps you anticipate how your cash flow, profitability and funding need are impacted.

Calculate Net Present value of the venture

Net present value (NPV) is the difference between the present value of cash inflows and the present value of cash outflows over a period of time. NPV is used in capital budgeting and investment planning to analyze the profitability of a projected investment or project.

The following formula is used to calculate NPV:

$$NPV = \sum_{t=1}^{n} \frac{R_t}{(1+i)^t}$$

where:

R_t = Net cash inflow-outflows during a single period t

i = Discount rate or return that could be earned in alternative investments

t = Number of timer periods

A positive net present value indicates that the projected earnings generated by a project or investment - in present dollars - exceed the anticipated costs, also in present dollars. It is assumed that an investment with a positive NPV will be profitable, and an investment with a negative NPV will result in a net loss. This concept is the basis for the Net Present Value Rule, which dictates that only investments with positive NPV values should be considered.

NET PRESENT VALUE OF FUTURE CASH FLOW					
INT	YRS	CF		PVF	CF*PVF
10%	1	$	15,00,000	0.909	$ 13,63,636
	2	$	15,00,000	0.826	$ 12,39,669
	3	$	15,00,000	0.751	$ 11,26,972
	4				$ -
	5				$ -
		$	45,00,000	NPV	$ 37,30,278

With the investment of $ 1 Million and Net Present Value of the venture is $3.7 Million, it state that, this is a good venture to invest in.

Calculate Internal Rate of Return of the venture

The internal rate of return (IRR) is a metric used in capital budgeting to estimate the profitability of potential investments. The internal rate of return is a discount rate that makes the net present value (NPV) of all cash flows from a particular project equal to zero. IRR calculations rely on the same formula as NPV does. It is important for a business to look at the IRR as the plan for future growth and expansion. The formula and calculation used to determine this figure follows.

$$0 = \text{NPV} = \sum_{t=1}^{T} \frac{C_t}{(1+IRR)^t} - C_0$$

where:

C_t = Net cash inflow during the period t
C_0 = Total initial investment costs
IRR = The internal rate of return
t = The number of time periods

Year	Cash Flows
0	-10,00,000
1	15,00,000
2	15,00,000
3	15,00,000
4	
5	

Discount Rate	10%
IRR	139%

In this case, the IRR is 139%. Given the assumption of a weighted average cost of capital (WACC) of 10%, the venture adds value.

Q&A

- What all the risk in investing in venture?
- Your Answer :

- When venture get fund and at what time horizon?
- Your Answer :

- What will be a deal for funding?
- Your Answer :

- The amount to raise?
- Your Answer :

- Who are the investor ?
- Your Answer :

- What will be a term for funding ?
- Your Answer :

- Make a financial Model for three years for your venture?
- Your Answer:-

- Does your venture have positive net profit?
- Your Answer:-

- Does your venture have positive Cash Flow?
- Your Answer:-

- Does your venture NPV is greater than cash flow?
- Your Answer:-

- Does your venture investment is less than net present value?
- Your Answer:-

- Does your venture IRR is greater than cost of capital (WACC)?
- Your Answer:-

- What you will for that? To pick the right people to execute on a compelling idea that offers sufficient

value creation and capture potential to justify taking on the risk, structure deals that attract, motivate, and retain the right employees, investors, suppliers, and customers?
- *Your Answer:-*

There are no guarantees. Ventures fail for many reasons, some internal and some external. When ventures fail, it doesn't necessarily mean the people have failed. People only fail if they lie, cheat, or steal or if they consistently make the wrong decisions.

Case Study Facebook Funding

Facebook is a social networking service launched as The Facebook on February 4, 2004. It was founded by Mark Zuckerberg with his college roommates and fellow Harvard University students Eduardo Saverin, Andrew McCollum, Dustin Moskovitz and Chris Hughes. The website's membership was initially limited by the founders to Harvard students, but was expanded to other colleges in the Boston area, the Ivy League, and gradually most universities in the United States and Canada, corporations, and by September 2006, to everyone with a valid email address along with an age requirement of being 13 and older.

Initial funding

Facebook was initially incorporated as a Florida LLC. For the first few months after its launch in February 2004, the costs for the website operations for thefacebook.com were paid for by Mark Zuckerberg and Eduardo Saverin, who had taken equity stakes in the company. The website also ran a few advertisements to meet its operating costs.

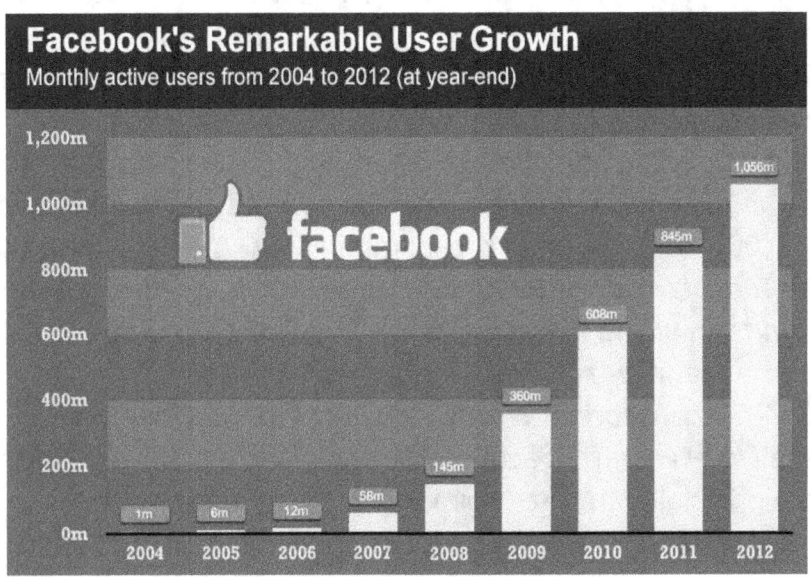

First angel investment

In the summer of 2004, venture capitalist Peter Thiel made a $500,000 angel investment in the social network Facebook for 10.2% of the company and joined Facebook's board. This was the first outside investment in Facebook.

In his book The Facebook Effect, David Kirkpatrick outlines the story of how Thiel came to make his investment: former Napster and Plaxo employee Sean Parker, who at the time had assumed the title of "President" of Facebook, was seeking investors for Facebook. Parker approached Reid Hoffman, the CEO of work-based social network LinkedIn. Hoffman liked Facebook but declined to be the lead investor because of the potential for conflict of interest with his duties as LinkedIn CEO.

He redirected Parker to Peter Thiel, whom he knew from their PayPal days (both Hoffman and Thiel are considered members of the PayPal Mafia). Thiel met Parker and Mark Zuckerberg, the Harvard college student who had founded Facebook and controlled it. Thiel and Zuckerberg got along well and Thiel agreed to lead Facebook's seed round with $500,000 for 10.2% of the company. **(if Thiel's 10% of the company is worth $500,000, then 100% of the company should be worth $5 million, or $500,000 divided by 10%).** Hoffman and Mark Pincus also participated in the round, along with Maurice Werdegar who led the investment on behalf of Western Technology Investment. The investment was originally in the form of a convertible note, to be converted to equity if Facebook reached 1.5 million users by the end of 2004. Although Facebook narrowly missed the target, Thiel allowed the loan to be converted to equity anyway. Thiel said of his investment:

I was comfortable with them pursuing their original vision. And it was a very reasonable valuation. I thought it was going to be a pretty safe investment.

Q&A

- Why face book need such valuation?
- Your Answer :

- Why Peter Thiel paid $500,000 with valuation of $5 Million? if you're as a angel investor
- Your Answer :

- Would you have made the same payment as Peter Thiel did as angel investor?
- Your Answer :

Accel investment (Series A)

In April 2005, Accel Partners agreed to make a $12.7 million venture capital investment in a deal that valued Facebook at $98 million. Accel joined Facebook's board, and the board was expanded to five seats, with Zuckerberg, Thiel, and Breyer in three of the seats, and the other two seats currently being empty but with Zuckerberg free to nominate anybody to those seats.

Greylock investment (Series B)

In April 2006, Facebook closed its Series B funding round. This included $27.5 million from a number of venture capitalists, including Greylock Partners and Meritech Capital, plus additional investments from Peter Thiel and Accel Partners. The valuation for this round was about $500 million.

A leaked cash flow statement showed that during the 2005 fiscal year, Facebook had a net gain of $5.66 million.

For your venture you need to identifying opportunity and raising money, your goal in every business is to find potentially valuable opportunities and to turn possibilities into reality. In the very beginning, as at facebook believed they would capture the opportunity to create value to the customer, it is same applicable in all the business.

Calculate the Value of Your Investment

CASE A

Investment	$100000
50 % Chance of venture caluation will be	$1 Million
80% Change Venture fail & will be	$0
Discount Rate	0

Expected value of the investment:

($1, 000,000 * 20%) + ($0 * 80%) = $200,000/-

The expected value of cash flow where 80% chance is the venture might fail.
To get a Net Present Value of the investment:-

Expected Future Cash Flow is = $200,000 – Investment $100,000 = $100,000

Example
VALUATION OF COMPANY
    20% = $ 25,000.00

VALUE OF COMPANY $ 1,25,000.00

Q&A

- *If you want to invest in this venture $100,000 and you raise fund, what percentage you need to give to the investor?*
- *Your Answer*

The Answer is 50 % as the expected cash flow is $200,000, to raise fund, you need to value the company for $200,000 and if investor invest $100,000 it will be 50 % of the equity.

CASE B

Investment	$100000
50 % Chance of venture calcuation will be	$1 Million
50% Change Venture fail & will be	$0
Discount Rate	0

Expected value of the investment:

($1, 000,000 * 50%) + ($0 * 50%) = $500,000/-

The expected value of cash flow where 50% chance is the venture might fail.

To get a Net Present Value of the investment:-

Expected Future Cash Flow is = $500,000 – Investment $100,000 = $400,000

Q&A

- If you want to invest in this venture $100,000 and you raise fund, what percentage you need to give to the investor?
- Your Answer

The Answer is 50 % as the expected cash flow is $500,000, to raise fund, you need to value the company for $500,000 and if investor invest $100,000 it will be 20 % of the equity.

Before making any kind of investment, it is very important to do the test, if you test is successful and there is a chance to succeed is 50 % or 80 %, than your shareholding in the venture will be high such as:

- If the valuation of the venture increase subject to the success rate of the venture to be successful, your shareholding equity will be high as we have learn in CASE B

- If there is a question mark in the success rate of the venture then your equity shareholding will be less as we have learn in CASE A.

Why the venture Fail

In another study, CB Insights looked at the post-mortems of 101 start-ups to compile a list of the Top 20 Reasons Start-ups Fail. The focus was on company level reasons for failure. The top nine most significant from this study are:

- No market need
- Ran out of cash
- Not the right team
- Got outcompeted
- Pricing/cost issue
- Poor product
- Need/lack business model
- Poor marketing
- Ignore customers

Case Study

Beepi.com

looked like a promising venture on paper. The used car selling and buying marketplace was released at a time when such online marketplaces had a lot of potentials. They even managed to get $60 million Series B funding round.

It finally shut down in 2017 after being in business for over four years. The used car dealer DGDG tried to buy the startup but pulled out eventually.

What went wrong?

Beepi was a classic example of bad leadership and management. Some would say they went too big too soon. The founders were able to quickly raise a lot of money but did not spend it carefully. Apparently, the company was burning through $7 million monthly at one point just paying salaries which included very high salaries for top executives.

What lesson should you learn?

Money runs out eventually if you do not spend it carefully. Time and again, startups have failed because of running out money. For many it is simply bad luck, however, in the case of Beepi, it was bad management.

Google Glass

Google is one of the biggest companies in the world but it has its fair share of failures as well. Google Glass was a futuristic smart device by Google that brought a new twist to wearable technology. Even after much hype, it failed immediately.

What went wrong?

Perhaps it was a bit ahead of the time or it raised privacy concerns. Most importantly, it was super expensive for the masses. It just failed to connect with the consumers who did not see a much value in it.

What lesson should you learn?

Innovation is great as long as it benefits the consumers. Also, you have to do anything and everything including cutting costs to bring the price down if you want to sell your product. You need to set up a smart marketing strategy where you can offer discounts in a way that it benefits you as well as your customers.

The bottom line is that every failure has a lesson to teach. And it is better to learn from other people's mistakes than your own. Startups face an incredible amount of challenges and there is no magic formula for success. However, you can improve your chances by avoiding the obvious pitfalls.

It is quite clear from the examples above that even if you find investors and get all the funding you need, you might still fail. It is an ever changing world and you need to stay at the top of your game no matter what.

Calculate Free Cash Flow of the venture

Investors invest in companies that produce plenty of free cash flow (FCF). It signals a company's ability to pay debt, pay dividends, buy back stock and facilitate the growth of business - all important undertakings from an investor's perspective.

Free cash flow can be calculated as follows:

Element	Source
EBIT x (1-Tax rate)	Current Income Statement
+ Depreciation & Amortization	Current Income Statement
- Changes in Working Capital	Prior & Current Balance Sheets: Current Assets and Liability accounts
- Capital expenditure (CAPEX)	Prior & Current Balance Sheets: Property, Plant and Equipment accounts
= Free Cash Flow	

Free Cash Flow = Operating Cash Flow – Expenditures

The importance of strong cash flow is aptly stated in the common expression "cash is king." The premise of this is that having cash puts you in a more stable position with better buying power. While you can borrow money at times, cash affords you greater protection against loan defaults or foreclosures. Cash flow is distinct from cash position. Having cash on hand is critical, but cash flow indicates an ongoing ability to generate and use cash.

There are three major types of profit that analysts analyze: gross profit, operating profit, and net profit. Each type of profit gives the analyst more information about the company's performance, especially when compared against other time periods and industry competitors. All three levels of profitability can be found on the income statement.

A positive free cash flow indicates the company is creating more cash than is being spent to operate and grow the business. Conversely, a negative free cash flow, highlights the company is not generating enough money to properly support its business activities; meaning growth is not possible in the company's current state. Of course, this ought to be reviewed within the context of that company's situation – for example, some small businesses have negative free cash flow in their first several years before they really begin to take off.

Free cash flow is an especially important concept for companies that have gone public because businesses with a positive free cash flow have significantly more opportunities they can pursue that will enhance their value to shareholders. Without cash on hand, it becomes much harder for these companies to create new products, acquire new companies or intellectual properties, pay their dividends and reduce the amount of debt they owe.

In addition, many investors or venture capital no longer use net income to measure the financial performance of a company, opting instead to use free cash flow as their primary means of analysis. This is because it's much easier for companies to manipulate their data or provide misleading figures regarding their net worth than it is with free cash flow.

Case Study A

The Company A

In Million

Projected Growth Rate		10.00%	10.00%
Income Statement	Year 1	Year 2	Year 3
Sales	$100.00	$110.00	$121.00
Cost of Goods Sold	$40.00	$66.00	$72.60
Gross Margin	$40.00	$44.00	$48.40
Selling, General and Administrative	$20.00	$22.00	$24.20
Operating Profits	$20.00	$22.00	$24.20
Tax	$6.00	$6.60	$7.26
After-Tax Operating Profits	$14.00	$15.40	$16.94

Balance Sheet	Year 1	Year 2	Year 3
Assets			
Cash	$1.00	$1.10	$1.21
Excess Cash	$0.00	$11.80	$24.78
Inventory	$12.00	$13.20	$14.52
Accounts Receivable	$15.00	$16.50	$18.15
Net Property, Plant & Equipment (NPPE)	$20.00	$22.00	$24.20
Total Assets	$48.00	$64.60	$82.86
Liabilities			
Accounts Payable	$12.00	$13.20	$14.52
Shareholders' Equity	$36.00	$51.40	$68.34
Total Liabilities	$48.00	$64.60	$82.86

The company A is a new venture and the financial model state that company will generate revenue year one will be $ 100 Million , after two years in third year company projected $121 Million with $16.94 Million Net profit .

If you check Excess cash flow is year one is zero and year third is $24.78 Million that the excess cash generating from the revenue, let see further what the free cash flow is, if there is no free cash flow, there is an issue in the venture, it's going to be very tough to operate the venture smoothly.

Working Capital Schedule	Year 1	Year 2
Cash	$1.00	$1.10
Accounts Receivable	$15.00	$16.50
Inventory	$12.00	$13.20
Accounts Payable	$12.00	$13.20
Net Working Capital (NWC)	16.0	17.6
Change in NWC		1.6

Operating Cash Flow	Year 2
Net Earnings	$15.40
Plus: Depreciation & Amortization	
Less: Changes in Working Capital	1.6
Cash from Operations	$13.80
Investing Cash Flow	
Investments in Property & Equipment	2.00
Free Cash Flow [FCF]	$11.80

If you check working capital schedule the cash is increased to $1.10 Million and to calculate the operating cash flow, you need to add D&A and less changes in the working capital that is $1.6 Million for year second.

Once you will get the cash from operation is $13.8 Million, from investing cash flow subtract the investment in PPE is $2 Million and you will get FREE CASH FLOW is $11.8 Million.

If we check the cash flow for third year to know, what is the status of cash flow is it increasing or decreasing, let's calculate the free cash flow for third year.

Working Capital Schedule	Year 3
Cash	$1.21
Accounts Receivable	$18.15
Inventory	$14.52
Accounts Payable	$14.52
Net Working Capital (NWC)	19.4
Change in NWC	(10.0)

Operating Cash Flow	Year 3
Net Earnings	$16.94
Plus: Depreciation & Amortization	
Less: Changes in Working Capital	(10.0)
Cash from Operations	$26.98
Investing Cash Flow	
Investments in Property & Equipment	2.20
Free Cash Flow [FCF]	$24.78

There is a 10 % growth in the revenue in third year, the net earning is $16.94 million and subtract changes in working capital we will get positive $10 million, so we will add back with net earnings $26.78 Million, subtract the investments in PPE is $2.2 million, the FREE CASH FLOW is $ 24.78 Million .

The free cash flow as:

- For Year 2nd - $11.8 Million
- For Year 3rd -$24.78 Million

Free cash flow is important because it allows a company to pursue opportunities that enhance shareholder value. Without cash, it's tough to develop new products, make acquisitions, pay dividends and reduce debt. ... If these investments earn a high return, the strategy has the potential to pay off in the long run.

When you make a business plans, make sure you check the free cash flow, the rule of entrepreneur state that *"NEVER RUN OUT OF CASH"*

Q&A

- Positive Free cash flow is good or bad for venture?
- Your Answer :

Case Study B

IN MILLION

YEAR	GROWTH RATE	FREE CASH FLOW
1	2%	$ 10.00
2	5%	$ 0.15
3	4%	$ -10.00
4	7%	$ -20.00
5	6%	$ -0.05
6	10%	$ 0.10
7	12%	$ 20.00
8	18%	$ 25.00

The free cash flow is negative but the growth rate is positive, such as growth rate in the year four is 7% but the FCF is -$20 Million.

Q&A

- What could be the reason for negative cash flow, where there is a positive growth rate?

- Your Answer :

Although companies and investors usually want to see positive cash flow from all of a company's operations, having negative cash flow from investing activities is not always bad and needs further evaluation before decisions are made on a company's investing activities.

It's entirely possible and not uncommon for a growing company to have a negative cash flow from investing activities. For example, if a growing company decides to invest in long-term fixed assets, it will appear as a decrease in cash within that company's cash flow from investing activities.

Even well-established companies make investments in long-term assets such as property and equipment from time to time might and might cause investing activities to go negative.

The PPE have some assets classes such as:

Appreciating Assets

- Land
- Building

Depreciating Asset

- Plant & Equipments
- Vehicles
- Furniture and fixtures

Understanding how prospective land values influence property returns allows investors to make better choices. Land appreciates because it is limited in supply, consequently, as the population increases, so does the demand for land, driving its price up over time

A fully depreciated asset is a property, plant or piece of equipment (PP&E) which, for accounting purposes, is worth only its salvage value. Whenever an asset is capitalized, its cost is depreciated over several years according to a depreciation schedule.

If your venture is investing in land and building then , your investment is increasing , if in case venture find difficulty then you may sell and in cash .

Calculate Cash Conversion Cycle (CCC) of the venture

The cash conversion cycle (CCC) is a formula in management accounting that measures how efficiently a company's managers are managing its working capital. The CCC measures the length of time between a company's purchase of inventory and the receipts of cash from its accounts receivable. The CCC is used by management to see how long a company's cash remains tied up in its operations.

This metric takes into account how much time the company needs to sell its inventory, how much time it takes to collect receivables, and how much time it has to pay its bills without incurring penalties.

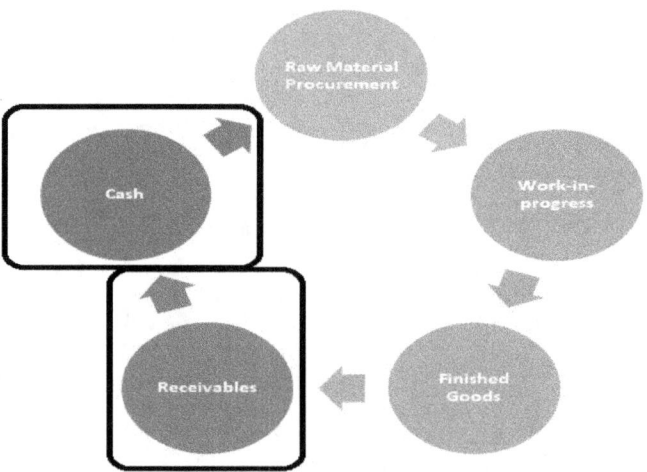

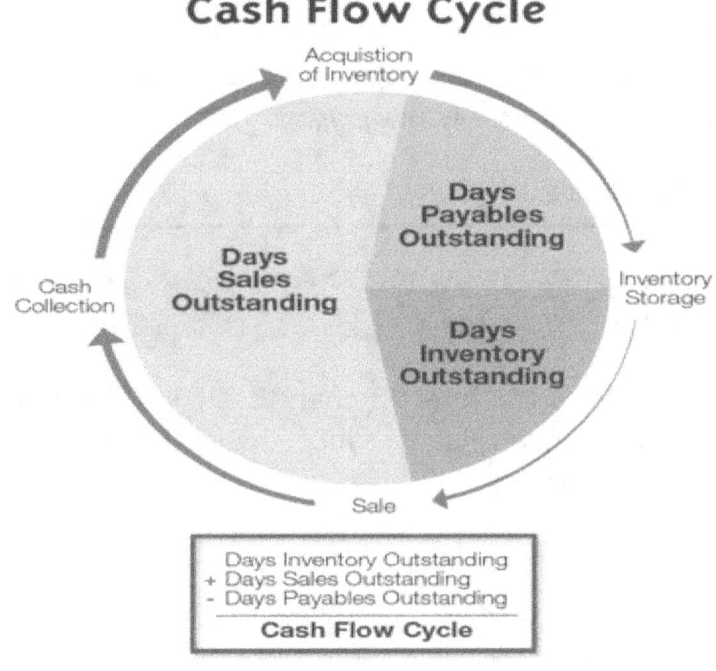

Case Study

TOTAL DEBTS	$100 Million
ACCOUNTS RECEIVABLE	$100 Million
DEBT INTEREST RATE ANNUALLY	12%
ACCOUNTS RECEIVABLE CREDIT DAYS	30

BILL DUE INTEREST COST FOR 30 DAYS	$	1,00,000.00
DEBT INTEREST RATE MONTHLY %		1%
DEBTS INTEREST CHARGES FOR 30 DAYS	$	10,000.00
2% CASH DISCOUNT TO ACCOUNT RECEIVABLE FOR 10 DAYS EARLY PAYMENT, INTEREST COST	$	6,667.00

Saved by the company if company offer 2 % discount to the account receivable for the early payment.

Company Saved from monthly early payment	$	93,333.00
Annually saving for a Company	$	11,19,996.00

Saved	$1.12 Million

Total saving from the interest charges is $1.12 Million , with this method company can reduce the cash flow cycle and generate more profit .

Q&A

- *Giving 2% discount is good or bad for venture?*
- *Your Answer :*

- *What do you think about this method is good or bad for venture?*
- *Your Answer :*

- *Can you apply this method in your venture?*
- *Your Answer :*

Calculate Burn Rate & Fume date of the venture

Burn rate is the rate at which a company is losing money.[citation needed] It is typically expressed in monthly terms. E.g., "the company's burn rate is currently $65,000 per month." In this sense, the word "burn" is a synonymous term for negative cash flow. It is also measure for how fast a company will use up its shareholder capital. If the shareholder capital is exhausted, the company will either have to start making a profit, find additional funding, or close down.

The burn rate is typically used to describe the rate at which a new company is spending its venture capital to finance overhead before generating positive cash flow from operations. It is a measure of negative cash flow.

The burn rate is usually quoted in terms of cash spent per month. For example, if a company is said to have a burn rate of $1 million, it would mean that the company is spending $1 million per month.

The burn rate is used by startup companies and investors to track the amount of monthly cash that a company spends before it starts generating its own income. A company's burn rate is also used as a measuring stick for its runway, the amount of time the company has before it runs out of money.

So, if a company has $1 million in the bank, and it spends $100,000 a month, its burn rate would be $100,000 and its runway would be 10 months, derived as:

($1,000,000) / ($100,000) = 10

```
Cash in Hand or Bank = $500000
Monthly Expenses    = $50000
Burn Rate is        = 5 Month
```

However, when the burn rate begins to exceed burn forecasts, or revenue fails to meet expectations, the usual recourse is to reduce the burn rate, regardless of money in the bank. This normally means reducing staff.

Burn rate is a concept that every entrepreneur must become familiar with. It's a key measure of sustainability, or how long your business can stay afloat until sales rise. Stated differently, how long can your company operate until you run out of money?

Q&A

- What is your burn rate for the venture?

- Your Answer :

- How long the cash will last?

- Your Answer :

Cash flow refers to generating or producing cash (cash inflows) and using or consuming cash (cash outflows). You should think of cash flow as the lifeblood of your business, and you must keep that blood circulating at all times in order avoid failure. Managing cash flows is essential to the successful operation of your business.

Fume date: Closely related to the burn rate, the fume date is an estimate of the date a company will run out of cash and be left running on fumes.

In other word fume date is the date when your cash will be vanish from the venture and the venture will left with zero cash ,so before the fume date , you need to get the additional funding for the start-up.

Source of funding of the venture

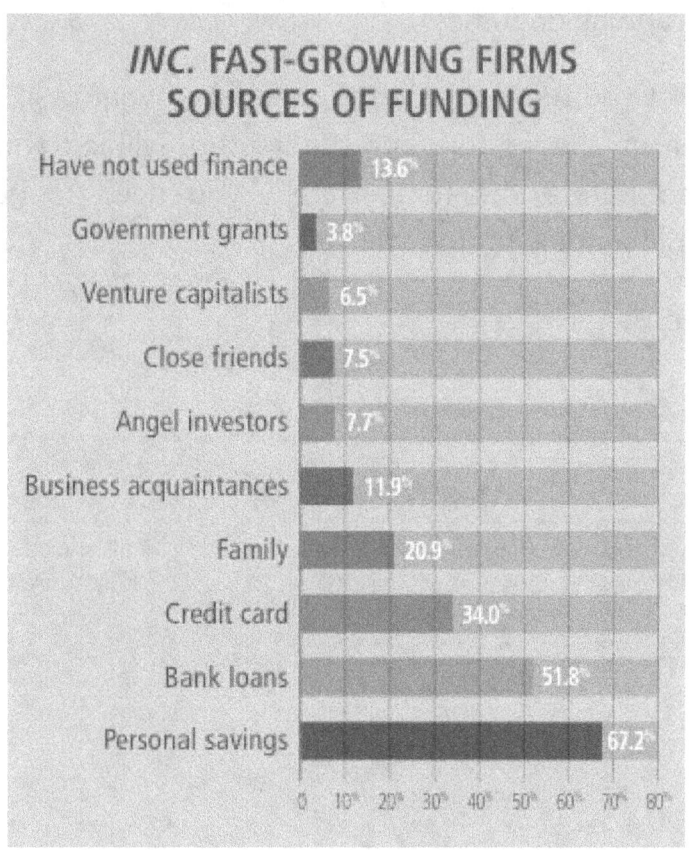

Sources of Financing for small business or start-up can be divided into two parts: Equity Financing and Debt Financing. Some common source of financing business is Personal investment, business angels, and assistant of government, commercial bank loans, financial bootstrapping, and buyouts. Let us discuss the sources of financing business in greater detail.

Personal investment

When starting a business, your first investor should be yourself—either with your own cash or with collateral on your assets. This proves to investors and bankers that you have a long-term commitment to your project and that you are ready to take risks.

When you have started your venture, you are the first one to fund the company initially from your saving and your retirement saving and from your parents retirement saving and as venture go on, you might require more fund and in this case you might ask more fund from your parents savings, when nobody else would fund you and only your family could fund your venture, you might put all your parents saving at risk, you could lost the money , that your parents plans to live on a comfortable life after retirement. You have to make your venture successful; don't invest in a venture, where the test shows that the ratio of losing your money is 80%.

Family & Friends Money

This is money loaned by a spouse, parents, family or friends. Investors and bankers consider this as "patient capital", which is money that will be repaid later as your business profits increase.

They may want to have equity in your business .A business relationship with family or friends should never be taken lightly. Obviously, friends and family can provide either equity or debt funding. While this may initially seem like a good source, be careful about selling part of your business to this group. Unfortunately, businesses fail. The loss of capital can then cause hurt feelings, ruins friendships and make for unpleasant family gatherings. Be sure that your investors know the true risks.

Venture capital

The first thing to keep in mind is that venture capital is not necessarily for all entrepreneurs. Right from the start, you should be aware that venture capitalists are looking for technology-driven businesses and companies with high-growth potential in sectors such as information technology, communications and biotechnology.

Venture capitalists take an equity position in the company to help it carry out a promising but higher risk project. This involves giving up some ownership or equity in your business to an external party. Venture capitalists also expect a healthy return on their investment, often generated when the business starts selling shares to the public. Be sure to look for investors who bring relevant experience and knowledge to your business.

Angels

Angels are generally wealthy individuals or retired company executives who invest directly in small firms owned by others. They are often leaders in their own field who not only contribute their experience and network of contacts but also their technical and/or management knowledge. Angels tend to finance the early stages of the business with investments in the order of $25,000 to $100,000.

Institutional venture capitalists prefer larger investments, in the order of $1,000,000.

In exchange for risking their money, they reserve the right to supervise the company's management practices. In concrete terms, this often involves a seat on the board of directors and an assurance of transparency.

Bank loans

Bank loans are the most commonly used source of funding for small and medium-sized businesses. Consider the fact that all banks offer different advantages, whether it's personalized service or customized repayment. It's a good idea to shop around and find the bank that meets your specific needs.

In general, you should know bankers are looking for companies with a sound track record and that have excellent credit. A good idea is not enough; it has to be backed up with a solid business plan. Start-up loans will also typically require a personal guarantee from the entrepreneurs.

Repayment Burden: Loan borrowers must make periodic payments to their banks. Those who fall behind on payments face the prospect of having their assets seized. Even if you manage to make late payments, your bank could still report you to credit bureaus – a move that negatively affects your credit score. With a lower score, obtaining loans in the future becomes more difficult. The repayment burden is a disadvantage compared to raising money through shareholders, because shareholders don't require regular repayments. Instead, they are typically paid dividends only on profits.

Irregular Payment Amounts: If you get a bank loan with a variable interest rate, the rate changes with market conditions. This makes it difficult to determine the exact amount of future payments. Consequently, it becomes challenging to make sound financial plans.

- Additional Burden on Cost of Goods
- Security Needs and Creditworthiness
- Partial Funding Requirement
- Strict Repayment Schedule
- Prepayment Penalties and Charges
- Interest Rate Risk / Cost of Funds
- Processing Fee
- Increased Compliances

Collateral is something you own that the bank can take if you fail to pay off your debt or loan. This can be any item of value that is accepted as an alternate form of repayment in case of default. If loan payments are not made, assets can be seized and sold by banks. This ensures that a lender receives full or partial compensation for any outstanding balance on a defaulted debt. Loans with pledged collateral are known as "secured loans," and are often required for most consumer loans.

What is Collateral?

Item of value pledged by a borrower to secure a loan.

Backup for loan repayment that adds security for a lender.

Asset that a bank can seize and sell if a borrower defaults on their debt.

Most financial assets that can be seized and sold for cash are considered acceptable collateral, although each type of loan has different requirements. For a standard mortgage or auto loan, the home or car itself is used as collateral. With high-value personal loans, valuable possessions like jewelry or paintings are also accepted. When companies and small businesses apply for loans, they often put up equipment or other physical assets as collateral.

Crowdfunding

Explanation: nowadays it is hard to imagine crowdfunding once didn't exist in the Dutch (and international) financing ecosystem. With crowdfunding, the "crowd" finances the funding need of a company. Usually crowdfunding is performed via an online platform where entrepreneurs offer investment opportunities on one side of the platform and on the other side of the platform a large group of people invest small amounts to meet the entrepreneur's investment need.

You need to make sure that your business is always careful when it comes to borrowing money. Loans can be great solutions for businesses that don't want the hassle that often comes with finding an investor or business partner. However, ensuring that you will be able to pay back the amount that you borrow is essential because your assets could be taken from you as collateral if you fail to make the repayments.

"My personal advice to you , try to avoid personal guarantees for debt like Collateral, if you take fund from bank, they will ask for Collateral, and it is very risky .Bank ask you to pledge personal assets such like your house and land and building, that is owned by you or your parents to fund your venture with the interest charges and repayment plans. I am sure that many entrepreneur have survived personal guarantees, but I have seen people lose their home and property and put their family at risk when the venture fails, think hard of all the things that might go wrong and try to avoid that kind of exposure"

Q&A

- *What is your personal goal with entrepreneurship? What would success look like?*
- *Your Answer :*
- *How much fund venture need for the fume date?*
- *Your Answer :*
- *If your venture cannot able to arrange fund before fume date, what can go wrong?*
- *Your Answer :*

- *How you and your team will define your venture successful?*

- Your Answer :

- *How your investors define your venture successful?*

- Your Answer :

- *What are the chances of the venture unsuccessful?*

- Your Answer :

Any investor only invest in your company , when they find probability of success , bank never fund in any venture that is risky , bank want a safe bet , but if any other sources of fund is infusing , they will check the find the target market, design the product, and create happy, repeat customers.

- *What do investors and your customers expect to get from you and your venture?*

- Your Answer :

Entrepreneurship is hard. You need lots of help on the journey. It's like trying to climb Mt. Everest – it takes lots of people, time and money to get to the top and back. Every financing and hiring decision you make and every major strategic move impacts the path and the outcome. You should be focused on improving your organization at every stage.

- *How do you think about the role of a board of directors in an entrepreneurial venture? How many people should be on the board? What backgrounds would you look for? How should you communicate with the board? How can they be helpful?*
- *Your Answer :*

Three Rules to make your venture successful

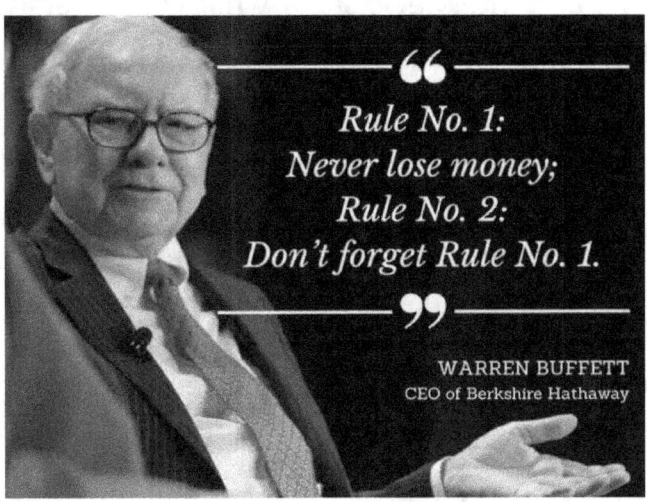

Right Opportunities Test

First, consider each aspect of your start-up. The questions you ask should help you dig deeper into your thought process and develop a plan. Resolving issues in the beginning will help you be successful.

These questions are examples of what you should think about before you start a business:

- Why do I want to start a business?
- What problem do I solve?
- Who is my target customer?
- What resources do I have?
- What are my goals?

A focus group involves a small number of consumers who use your offerings and provide feedback. Focus groups, surveys, and interviews show what consumers think before you go all in.

Although you're excited about your new business idea, you might want to wait a while before testing it, "Once I'm through that, the best way to test a business idea is to build some prototype and show it to people to get some honest and authentic feedback.

Introducing a new product or service without first testing the market is like jumping off a cliff into the sea, blindfolded-- unthinkable, life threatening, treacherous and unnecessarily risky. Many new ideas and products are successful because their creators identified an unmet need in the market and verified the viability of that concept.

Your time and money are extremely valuable to you--you can't afford to waste them by investing them in producing a product or service that fails in the marketplace. The more you test your product before you produce and sell it, the more likely you are to earn the sales and profits that you desire. Just remember, every dollar you spend in market testing will save you many dollars of losses later on in the marketing process.

- Develop a prototype, model or description of the product or service that you can show to others.
- Determine the price that you can sell the product for in the current marketplace.
- Go to a potential customer with your sample or prototype and ask if he would buy it.

- Compare your product with other products on the market.
- Visit trade shows and exhibitions--they're a terrific place to get immediate feedback on a new product.

Right People

The core values of a successful company are much more than a marketing ploy to show customers; they're a definition of what the company stands for and what its mission is, and you need to hire people who reflect these values.

Carefully define what you want your company to be, what you want the atmosphere at the office to be like, and what the ultimate mission of your company is. Once you've defined these core values, look for people who reflect them and who will get excited about moving the mission of your company forward.

A business is nothing without the people who work behind the scenes. While the entrepreneur may have big dreams, it is ultimately the team, with whose help he/she can realize the goals.

Hiring the right team is therefore extremely important for any business, and more so for a startup, since it is the team that plays a key role in understanding and executing the founder's vision.

Team Members

- Founder and co founder
- Investor
- Employee
- Customer

Founder and co founder

"A founder's individual characteristics are important but what's more important is that person's ability to bring a bigger and more experienced team with them," the researchers say. "And the bigger that team the more likely the firm will succeed."

Warren Buffett has been working with his long-time friend and business partner, Charlie Munger, for over 40 years. The two men have experienced unparalleled success together, building an investment business with more than $736 billion in assets. And, perhaps even more impressively, they've never had one argument.

"We've never had an argument in the entire time we've known each other, which is almost 60 years.

Investor

A person or any corporation who allocates capital to incorporation or startup with the agenda of financial return is an investor. There can be different types of investor, for instance mutual funds, hedge funds, Venture capital, angel investor etc. These investors can definitely help the start-up to raise capital for their businesses. Start-up can also elevate their capital from other sources, for example, shareholders fund (equity and preference both), long term borrowing, debentures, current liabilities, public fund, bank loan etc. However, there are degrees of risks involved for investing in a start-up. Not many investors will be in consonance with the idea of investing in a start-up. Opinions would differ. Some investor would have lackadaisical attitude as to not to fund the start-up whereas some would be willing to invest. Hence, the concept of angel investor and seed funding is prevalent in the current market. Angel investor also known as seed investor are affluent individual or entrepreneurs who renders capital for a business start-up, usually in quid pro quo of convertible debt or ownership equity or as agreed upon by the parties (as specified in the contract). Notwithstanding, in the context of business and risk management there are varied investor preferred over other as per the best options available to a start-up.

A term sheet is a non-binding document that lays out the proposed terms and conditions under which an investor (VC,angel or other) will make an equity investment in a startup.

What a term sheet does do is set out the broad parameters of a potential investment – a framework for negotiating the final agreement. What a term sheet does not do is bind an investor (or startup) to completing an investment in any legal manner (typically there are a number of additional documents that follow, including share purchase agreement, investor rights agreement, certificate of incorporation, ROFR and co-sale agreement, and voting agreement – that legally set the actual terms of the investment).

Employee

Building a capable and experienced team is one of the most crucial tasks of starting up. Investors believe that the risks would be lower if your team has good managerial skills, a nice chemistry, and a worthy prior experience in your domain.

Having a strong startup team is very crucial to the fate of your startup as its success ultimately lies on the shoulders of your team. Every team member should have an expertise in the department s/he's handling and an iron will to contribute to the fullest.

"My criteria to invest are the founders. So I won't check any business plans, any economic projections, spreadsheets; but (instead) I focus on the founder's mindset (and) passion." – Taizo Son, an investor in start-ups.

Berkshire's insurance businesses generated after-tax earnings of $1.4 billion from underwriting in 2016, an increase of $208 million from a year ago.

While the insurance business that Jain heads is a risky one, he doesn't expose the company to risk.

"His operation combines capacity, speed, decisiveness and, most important, brains in a manner unique in the insurance business,"

Buffett is so impressed with Jain that once he wrote to Jain's parents asking whether they have one more Ajit. The star was embarrassed when his parents framed the letter and hung it in the family living room in New Delhi.

How does one become so much loved by the god of investing?

"Buffett looks for managers who love their work and not money,"

Customer

A customer in the hand is worth two in the bush

The ancient proverb is apt here because data consistently supports the idea that retaining one happy customer is of much greater value than chasing half a dozen prospects. Research shows that winning over a new customer costs up to seven times more than keeping an existing one. Also, increasing customer retention rates by just five percent can increase profits by anywhere from 25 to 95 percent.
It must be evident now that customer development is crucial to the success of any new venture. An idea is great, but ideas don't always translate into viable businesses in the real world! Customer development allows you to see if the idea can in fact work.

But customer development isn't easy. It involves talking to those potential customers and gathering feedback, which means a lot of time and resources that might end up not turning into an actual business. But don't let that stop you from using this valuable method.
It might cost money to see if the idea even has legs, but it'll cost a lot more money if you develop an idea that has no customers. You must invest, of course, but that investment

must be done smartly. The time and resources spent to discern the value of moving forward is a wise investment.

Finance

"Never run out of cash"

If cash flow is the lifeblood of the business, then an investment round is a blood transfusion. It gets cash into the system when it's missing, but it's always going to stop at some point. That's something that founders need to take into account.

Developing a cash flow projection will enable you plan your working capital better in order to ensure that you pay your startups operational expenses on time as well as maintain a strong positive cash flow record, which will ultimately make it appealing to creditors.

Having a perpetually cash flow record will also accord your startup the ability to invest more capital in expansion by acquiring new employees, better equipment or even opening up new subsidiaries which will go a long way in propelling the startup to the next stage of growth and away from the financial woes associated with being a startup company.

Cash is definitely the king when it comes to the financial management of a growing company. The time gap between paying the suppliers/employees and learning from customers is the problem. An accurate cash flow projection can alert the entrepreneur against the trouble well before it strikes. This will help them in managing their cash flow as well as their receivables.

The basic idea is to improve the speed with which they would turn the materials and supplies into products, inventory into receivables, and receivables into cash. Even after playing smart and safe, an entrepreneur might foresee a situation where he/she lacks the cash to pay the bills.

This doesn't mean one has failed as a businessperson. It's just that he/she couldn't predict the future perfectly. In an ideal scenario, a startup should have enough cash to sustain for 6 months expenses. It eases the pressure on the entrepreneur and he can focus on the product delivery.

Blueprint of Billionaire Mind

"Your time is limited, so don't waste it living someone else's life. Don't be trapped by dogma – which is living with the results of other people's thinking. Don't let the noise of other's opinions drown out your own inner voice. And most important, have the courage to follow your heart and intuition. They somehow already know what you truly want to become. Everything else is secondary."

- Steve Jobs

8

Steve Jobs

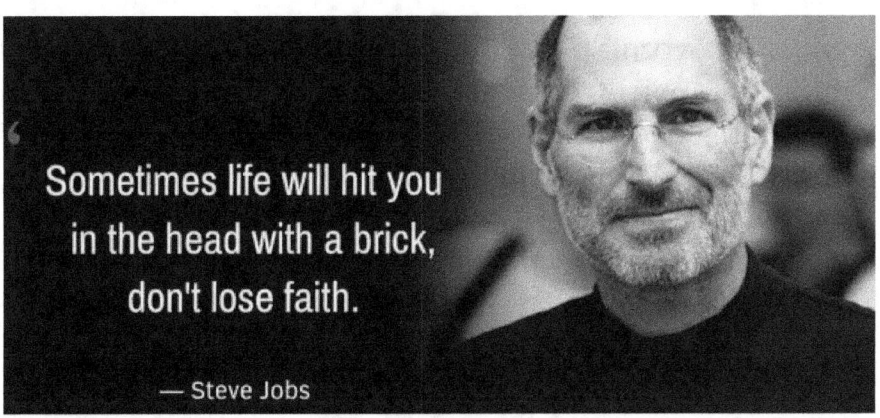

Biography

Steven Paul Jobs (February 24, 1955 – October 5, 2011) was an American business magnate, industrial designer, investor, and media proprietor. He was the chairman, chief executive officer (CEO), and co-founder of Apple Inc., the chairman and majority shareholder of Pixar, a member of The Walt Disney Company's board of directors following its acquisition of Pixar, and the founder, chairman, and CEO of NeXT. Jobs is widely recognized as a pioneer of the personal computer revolution of the 1970s and 1980s, along with Apple co-founder Steve Wozniak.

Jobs was born in San Francisco, California, and put up for adoption. He was raised in the San Francisco Bay Area. He attended Reed College in 1972 before dropping out that same year, and traveled through India in 1974 seeking enlightenment and studying Zen Buddhism. His declassified FBI report states that he used marijuana and LSD while he was in college, and once told a reporter that taking LSD was "one of the two or three most important things" he had done in his life.

Jobs and Wozniak co-founded Apple in 1976 to sell Wozniak's Apple I personal computer. Together the duo gained fame and wealth a year later with the Apple II, one of the first highly successful mass-produced microcomputers. Jobs saw the commercial potential of the Xerox Alto in 1979, which was mouse-driven and had a graphical user interface (GUI). This led to the development of the unsuccessful Apple Lisa in 1983, followed by the breakthrough Macintosh in 1984, the first mass-produced computer with a GUI. The Macintosh introduced the desktop publishing industry in 1985 with the addition of the Apple LaserWriter, the first laser printer to feature vector graphics. Jobs was forced out of Apple in 1985 after a long power struggle with the company's board and its then-CEO John Sculley. That same year, Jobs took a few of Apple's members with him to found NeXT, a computer platform development company that specialized in computers for higher-education and business markets. In addition, he helped to develop the visual effects industry when he funded the computer graphics division of George Lucas's Lucasfilm in 1986. The new company was Pixar, which produced the first 3D computer animated film Toy Story (1995).

Apple acquired NeXT in 1997, and Jobs became CEO of his former company within a few months. He was largely responsible for helping revive Apple, which had been at the verge of bankruptcy. He worked closely with designer Jony Ive to develop a line of products that had larger cultural ramifications, beginning in 1997 with the "Think different" advertising campaign and leading to the iMac, iTunes, iTunes Store, Apple Store, iPod, iPhone, App Store, and the iPad. In 2001, the original Mac OS was replaced with a completely new Mac OS X, based on NeXT's NeXTSTEP platform, giving the OS a modern Unix-based foundation for the first time. Jobs was diagnosed with a pancreatic neuroendocrine tumor in 2003. He died of respiratory arrest related to the tumor at age 56 on October 5, 2011.

Blueprint

There were many personality traits that helped Steve Jobs become the most successful entrepreneur of our time. We can all learn a lot from him. In addition, whether or not you've already reached success, Steve Jobs provides a fantastic blueprint to follow.

Magical thinking, Reality distortion field. Steve Jobs and Entrepreneurs both have this thinking. They are dreamers, they envision a better world of improved services and products. Einstein said "Imagination is more important than knowledge." They try to see things not as they are but how they could be.

If you don't love it, if you're not having fun doing it, you don't really love it, you're going to give up. – Steve Jobs

"I'm convinced that about half of what separates successful entrepreneurs from the non successful ones is pure perseverance." – Steve Jobs

Develop the Passion

Steve Jobs had both passion and self-confidence to turn his dream into a reality. You need to love what you're doing. Developing a strong passion for your work helps you on the road to success in business.

Stay Focused

From a small garage to becoming the world most valuable company, Apple Inc. has come a long way. It is due to the unflinching determination and laser focus of its founder, Steve Jobs. He was clear about what he wanted to achieve and stay focused throughout the journey. Sharing his secrets of success, he said, "That's been one of my mantras – focus and simplicity."

Learn, Learn, Learn

Steve Jobs proved that you do not need college degrees to make your business successful. Instead, he recommends a holistic approach to learning. Be a life-long learner and learn from any source you can come across. Rather than trying to learn everything about everything, you should focus your efforts on a specific subject and become an expert in that domain.

Seek Expert Advice

Even a visionary, like Steve Jobs, looks towards experts and opinion leaders for inspiration, wisdom and sound advice on how to improve. Young entrepreneurs should also follow in the footstep of the Apple's founder and seek expert advice. Before they do that, it is important to identify areas that need improvement, and then seek expert advice on how to make things better.

Look Into the Crystal Ball

What gives Apple an edge over its competitors was Steve's ability to be proactive and predict the future. His clairvoyance enabled him to predict what the future is going to be like and how technology is going to affect our lives. And this visionary outlook gave all Apple products a clear advantage over their competitors when it comes to innovation.

Young entrepreneurs can easily get a competitive advantage over their competitors if they're able to predict what sort of future problems are going to arise and exactly which ones your business can solve . Getting a sneak peek into the future will also help you in dealing with issues that might come in your way. Steve Jobs quoted Wayne Gretzky when he said, "I skate to where the puck is going to be, not where it has been."

Quality Over Quantity

Although most large organizations and startups focus on sales numbers (quantity) but Steve Jobs has a different take on things. He urges young entrepreneurs to go for quality rather than quantity. His words also reflect his approach when he said, "Quality is much better than quantity. One home run is much better than two doubles."

Give attention to detail, aim for perfection and deliver a quality product to your customers. Steve Jobs sums it up brilliantly when he said. "Design is not just what it looks like and feels like. Design is how it works." When you manage to achieve this feat, sales numbers will increase automatically.

Consider Failure as a Learning Opportunity

When Steve Jobs was invited to speak at Stanford University on commencement in 2005, he shared his story, "I didn't see it then, but it turned out that getting fired from Apple was the best thing that could have ever happened to me. The heaviness of being successful was replaced by the lightness of being a beginner again, less sure about everything. It freed me to enter one of the most creative periods of my life."

Instead of fearing failure, you should consider it as a learning opportunity as Steve Jobs did all his life and set an example for young entrepreneurs to follow. Identify the reasons for your failure with the help of project management software and a good mentor fix the issues. If you use failure as a source of motivation to improve upon your weaknesses, then success will come your way.

Take Risks

None of us might have developed an iPhone, if I was in Steve Jobs' shoes, especially, when it would left a dent on the sales of iPod. But Steve Jobs worked on it and succeeded in making Apple a pioneer in the smartphone market. That is what makes him stand out from the crowd. As a budding entrepreneur who wants to achieve ambitious goals, you should always be prepared to take risks but should be calculated risks. Take your time, think about both the pros and cons, and then make a decision.

Your Time Is Limited

Steve Jobs give aspiring young entrepreneurs a formula for overcoming fear and embarrassment of failure when he said, "Remembering that I'll be dead soon is the most important tool I've ever encountered to help me make the big choices in life. Because almost everything — all external expectations, all pride, all fear of embarrassment or failure – these things just fall away in the face of death, leaving only what is truly important."

Life is short and your time is limited so make it count instead of wasting it by pretending to be someone else. That is the message Steve Jobs gave to the world when he said, "Your time is limited; don't waste it living someone else's life. Do not be trapped by dogma, which is living the result of other people's thinking. Do not let the noise of other opinions drown your own inner voice. Most importantly, have the courage to follow your heart and intuition, they somehow already know what you truly want to become. Everything else is secondary."

Always remember you are not immortal

While addressing the students at Stanford University, Jobs said "Remembering that I'll be dead soon is the most important tool I've ever encountered to help me make the big choices in life. Because of almost everything — all external expectations, all pride, all fear of embarrassment or failure–these things just fall away in the face of death, leaving only what is truly important."

Whenever you feel depressed, confused, embarrassed or have any negative feelings, only remember one thing; you are not immortal. You will be dead soon, so instead of feeling depressed make sure that you utilize every second of life.

Though Steve Jobs has passed away, his legacy will be with us forever. He was an inspiring human being who was and is respected by many. The way he lived his life both personally and professionally is commendable and if we can learn from his teachings, then it will definitely help us in achieving success in life.

Don't let money define your existence

"Bottom line is, I didn't return to Apple to make a fortune. I've been very lucky in my life and already have one. When I was 25, my net worth was $100 million or so. I decided then that I wasn't going to let it ruin my life. There's no way you could ever spend it all, and I don't view wealth as something that validates my intelligence."

"My favorite things in life don't cost any money. It's really clear that the most precious resource we all have is time."

"Being the richest man in the cemetery doesn't matter to me. Going to bed at night saying we've done something wonderful, that's what matters to me."

See the silver lining in every dark cloud

"No one wants to die. Even people who want to go to heaven don't want to die to get there. And yet death is the destination we all share. No one has ever escaped it. And that is as it should be, because Death is very likely the single best invention of Life. It is Life's change agent. It clears out the old to make way for the new."

"I didn't see it then, but it turned out that getting fired from Apple was the best thing that could have ever happened to me. The heaviness of being successful was replaced by the lightness of being a beginner again, less sure about everything. It freed me to enter one of the most creative periods of my life."

9
Warren Buffett

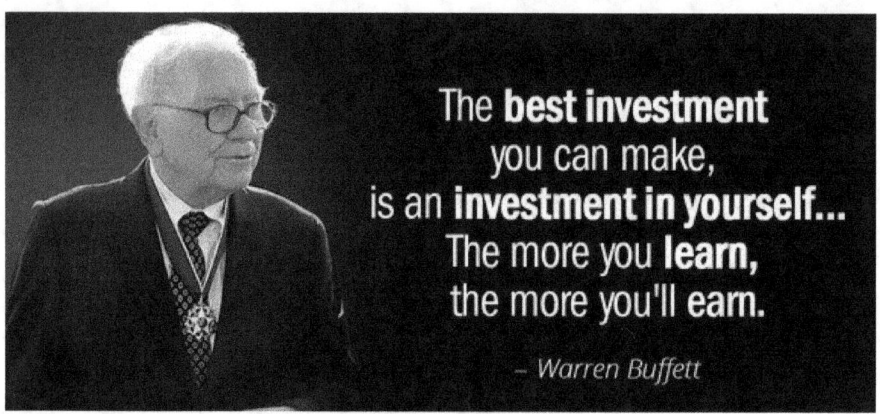

Biography

Warren Edward Buffett born August 30, 1930 is an American investor, business tycoon, and philanthropist, who is the chairman and CEO of Berkshire Hathaway. He is considered one of the most successful investors in the world[3][4] and has a net worth of US$88.9 billion as of December 2019, making him the fourth-wealthiest person in the world.

Buffett was born in Omaha, Nebraska. He developed an interest in business and investing in his youth, eventually entering the Wharton School of the University of Pennsylvania in 1947 before transferring and graduating from the University of Nebraska at the age of 19. He went on to graduate from Columbia Business School, where he molded his investment philosophy around the concept of value investing that was pioneered by Benjamin Graham. He attended New York Institute of Finance to focus his economics background and soon after began various business partnerships, including one with Graham. He created Buffett Partnership, Ltd in 1956 and his firm eventually acquired a textile manufacturing firm called Berkshire Hathaway, assuming its name to create a diversified holding company. In 1978, Charlie Munger joined Buffett and became vice-chairman of the company.

Buffett has been the chairman and largest shareholder of Berkshire Hathaway since 1970.[8] He has been referred to as the "Oracle" or "Sage" of Omaha by global media outlets.[9][10] He is noted for his adherence to value investing and for his personal frugality despite his immense wealth.[11] Research published at the University of Oxford characterizes Buffett's investment methodology as falling within "founder centrism" – defined by a deference to managers with a founder's mindset, an ethical disposition towards the shareholder collective, and an intense focus on exponential value creation. Essentially, Buffett's concentrated investments shelter managers from the short-term pressures of the market.

Buffett is a notable philanthropist, having pledged to give away 99 percent of his fortune to philanthropic causes, primarily via the Bill & Melinda Gates Foundation. He founded The Giving Pledge in 2009 with Bill Gates, whereby billionaires pledge to give away at least half of their fortunes.

Blueprint

Invest wisely

Buffett chooses to invest in ideas, not the people behind them. He once famously said that he chooses companies that are so wonderful, even an idiot could run them, mentioning the likelihood that someday one will.

Know what a good company looks like.

The list of essential characteristics Buffett looks for in an investment is surprisingly short. He wants a business that's easy to understand, with a consistent operating history; good long term prospects, possibly due to some durable competitive advantages, or "moats"; a trustworthy, high-quality management team; and solid financials: high margins, high return on equity, and high free cash flow. He does like growth, but less so than investors who are focused on the short term, since it's the nature of capitalism for growth not to last more than a few years as outsize profits attract fierce competition. When asked what metrics he uses in his investment decisions, his response is that if a computer could do valuation then everyone could do it, and if everyone could do it then the market would be efficient and there would be no bargains. Number geeks want math to provide easy answers, but it doesn't. Buffett's style of investing is at least as much art as science.

Life Comes Down to Decisions

Success is about consistency and learning every day. Buffett, a learning machine, reads six hours per day and wishes he could read more. Another valuable lesson in life and investing: long term, long term, long term! It's not a horse race—look for people and partnerships who also aim for the long term.

Do work that you love

Success comes when you do what you love. Warren Buffett lives by this rule and urges us all to live by it too. When you do what you love and are passionate about it, he says, you'll never work a day in your life.

"There comes the time when you ought to start doing what you want. Take a job that you love. You will jump out of bed in the morning. I think you are out of your mind if you keep taking jobs that you don't like because you think it will look good on your resume. Isn't that a little like saving up sex for your old age?"

Understand your business to the core

If there's anything Warren Buffett understands to the core; it's Berkshire Hathaway. Why? The reason is because he has been in the financial services industry for years and has a wealth of experience running Berkshire Hathaway. When the dot com boom began; many entrepreneurs and companies were jumping to start their own web based business but Warren Buffett refused to budge because he doesn't understand the technology industry. He only understands financial service businesses and he has stuck to this industry.

"If you understood a business perfectly and the future of the business, you need very little in the way of a margin of safety."

Spell out the specifics of a deal beforehand

Even when you are dealing with friends and relatives, have all the specifics of the deal spelt out beforehand, including your monetary benefits. Your bargaining leverage is always greatest before you begin a job—that's when you have something to offer that the other party wants.

"I am a better investor because I am a businessman and a better businessman because I am an investor."

Pick your associates carefully

Warren Buffett's success in business and investing can be attributed to his long standing friendship and partnership with Charlie. Entering into partnership is like marrying a wife; if things don't go as planned, it might leave a bitter taste in your mouth. So pick a partner who you have a long standing friendship with; pick a partner with a positive mindset and most importantly, choose a partner whose strengths complement your weaknesses.

"It is better to hang out with people better than you. Pick out associates whose behavior is better than yours and you will drift in that direction."

Assess the risk involved

Think about the worst and best possible scenarios and promptly make the most rational, progressive decision. That's basically the advice Buffett gave his son, Howie, when the FBI accused the younger Buffett of price-fixing in 1995. Howie quickly realized that the risks of staying in his then troubled company far outweighed any potential gains, and so he quit the next day. Assessing risks carefully helps you see where you are struggling and can guide you to make smarter decisions.

"I don't look to jump over seven-foot bars; I look around for one-foot bars that I can step over."

Limit your borrowing and what you owe others

Warren Buffett has never borrowed excessively, even when he was starting out in business. He says, "Nothing sedates rationality like large doses of effortless money." He has always negotiated with creditors to pay what he can, and when he is debt-free, saved his money to invest. Living on handouts, loans and credit cards will not make you rich.

"I have pledged – to you, the rating agencies and myself – to always run Berkshire with more than ample cash. We never want to count on the kindness of strangers in order to meet tomorrow's obligations. When forced to choose, I will not trade even a night's sleep for the chance of extra profits."

Think long term

The reason most businesses fail is because the entrepreneur or management is too short term focused. Warren Buffett is still alive at the time of this writing but he has already drawn a long term plan that will guide Berkshire Hathaway after his demise. Warren Buffett doesn't invest in a business that has no long term plan because he isn't investing for short term.

"Focus on your customers and lead your people as though their lives depend on your success."

Exercise vigilance over every expense and spending

Warren Buffett is well-known for being frugal and encouraging others to do so. He's lived in the same house he bought when he was 28 for a mere $31,500 to date. Being frugal and conservative with your spending helps you avoid waste. And when you avoid waste, you make your money work for you and save enough to invest for the future.

"If you buy things you do not need, soon you will have to sell things you need."

Know when to quit

Warren Buffett makes mistakes just like any one of us, but he learns from his mistakes and doesn't repeat them. Know when to walk away from a loss. And remember in businesses and in people, better quality businesses are more likely to grow and compound cash flow; low quality businesses often erode.

"You only have to do a very few things right in your life so long as you don't do too many things wrong."

Be consistent and patient

Warren Buffett says, "Time is the friend of the wonderful business, the enemy of the mediocre." The long and rocky road to success holds many valuable lessons and makes victory that much sweeter. So, be patient and keep pressing on. Don't obsess over quick results and instant gratification. Success doesn't come overnight—not even for Warren Buffett.

"No matter how great the talent or efforts, some things just take time. You can't produce a baby in one month by getting nine women pregnant."

Reinvest your profits

In high school, Warren Buffet and a friend bought a pinball machine and put it to work in a barbershop. With the money they earned, they bought more machines until they had eight of them in different shops. The friends later sold the venture and Mr. Buffett used his proceeds to buy stocks and the rest to start another business. By the time he was 26, he had amassed $174,000, which is equivalent to about 1.4 million in today's value.

Look broadly for investment opportunities and reinvest like you have a single lifetime "punch card" with only 20 punches—make each one count. Even a small investment can generate great wealth if you are diligent enough to favor substance over form.

"I try to buy stock in businesses that are so wonderful that an idiot can run them. Because, sooner or later, one will."

Know the Terms of the Business

Understand the conditions attached to any business before venturing into it. If you are doing a work, know your pay; if you are combining to startup a business, know your ownership percentage/shareholding. Warren Buffett learned this lesson the hard way as a kid, when his grandfather Ernest hired him and a friend to dig out the family grocery store after a blizzard. The boys spent five hours shoveling until they could barely straighten their frozen hands. Afterward, his grandfather gave the pair less than 90 cents to split. Warren Buffett was horrified that he performed such backbreaking work only to earn pennies an hour. Always nail down the specifics of a deal in advanced even with your friends and relatives.

Be Persistent

Be determined to achieve your defined goal. Do not allow the success of your competitors deter you own startup. If you are diligent and committed, you will become a strong competitor in no time. Warren Buffett acquired the Nebraska Furniture Mart in 1983 because he liked the way its founder, Rose Blumkin, did business. A Russian immigrant, she built the mart from a pawnshop into the largest furniture store in North America. Her strategy was to undersell the big shots, and she was a merciless negotiator. To Warren Buffett, Rose embodied the unwavering courage that makes a winner out of an underdog.

Do Not Overlook Small Expenses

Some entrepreneurs will label this as being stingy with oneself but Warren Buffet admires friends that does everything within their means to check extra expenses. Buffett love investing in businesses run by managers who are obsessed over the tiniest costs. He once acquired a company whose owner counted the sheets in rolls of 500-sheet toilet paper to see if he was being cheated (he was). He also admired a friend who painted only one side of his office building that faced the road. Checking unnecessary expense can make your profits and pay check go much further.

Be Definite about what success is

You should understand what success is and know when you have attained success. Success to some entrepreneurs can mean reaching a target or making a certain amount of profit in a giving period but to Warren Buffet, it is not so. Despite his wealth, Warren Buffett does not measure success by dollars. In 2006, he pledged to give away almost his entire fortune to charities, primarily the Bill and Melinda Gates Foundation. He's adamant about not funding monuments to himself no Warren Buffett buildings or halls. "I know people who have a lot of money," he says, and they get testimonial dinners and hospital wings named after them. But the truth is that nobody in the world loves them. When you get to my age, you'll measure your success in life by how many of the people you want to have loved you, actually do love you. That's the ultimate test of how you've lived your life."

Surround Yourself with the Right People and Create a Culture That Rewards the Behavior You Want Emulated

The heavy lifting is done by Berkshire Hathaway's operating subsidiaries. Those businesses, many of which would be in the Fortune 500 if spun-off, are run by CEOs who show up to work each day. They manage truly global enterprises that produce billions and billions of surplus wealth that then gets shipped to Omaha twice a year. Though occasional problems pop up, which is bound to happen in a firm of its size, Buffett's talent for attracting great executives, making them want to win, and staying loyal to the business is too important to casually dismiss. In many businesses, the quality of the people doing the work is of the utmost importance to the profitability. Get better people, enjoy better results.

Likewise, be on the lookout for perverse incentives. You want to avoid creating compensation or recognition systems that cause employees, contractors, or other parties to engage in immoral, unethical, illegal, or otherwise questionable behavior. You get more of what you subsidize so subsidize wisely.

10

Charlie Munger

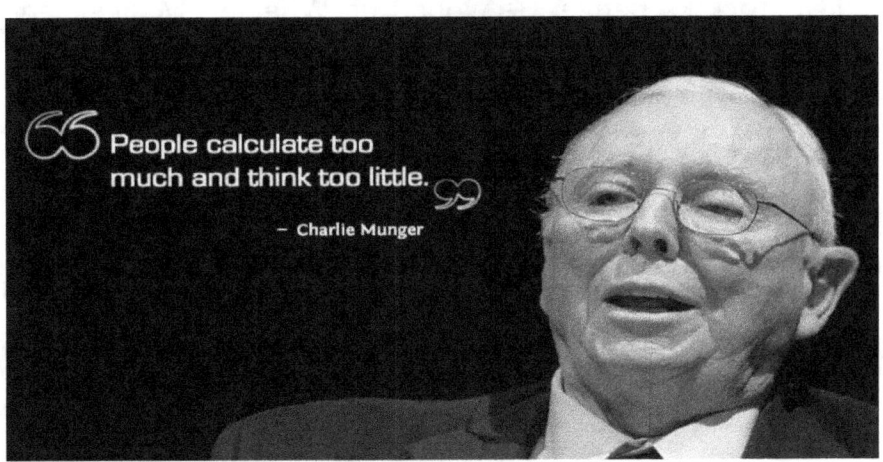

Biography

Charles Thomas Munger (born January 1, 1924) is an American investor, businessman, former real estate attorney, and philanthropist. He is vice chairman of Berkshire Hathaway, the conglomerate controlled by Warren Buffett; Buffett has described Munger as his partner. Munger served as chairman of Wesco Financial Corporation from 1984 through 2011. He is also chairman of the Daily Journal Corporation, based in Los Angeles, California, and a director of Costco Wholesale Corporation.

He moved with his family to California, where he joined the law firm Wright & Garrett (later Musick, Peeler & Garrett). In

1962 he founded and worked as a real estate attorney at Munger, Tolles & Olson LLP. He then gave up the practice of law to concentrate on managing investments and later partnered with Otis Booth in real estate development. He then partnered with Jack Wheeler to form Wheeler, Munger, and Company, an investment firm with a seat on the Pacific Coast Stock Exchange. He wound up Wheeler, Munger, and Co. in 1976, after losses of 32% in 1973 and 31% in 1974.

Although Munger is better known for his association with Buffett, he ran an investment partnership of his own from 1962 to 1975. According to Buffett's essay, "The Superinvestors of Graham-and-Doddsville", published in 1984, Munger's investment partnership generated compound annual returns of 19.8% during the 1962–75 period compared to a 5.0% annual appreciation rate for the Dow.

Munger was previously the chairman of Wesco Financial Corporation, now a wholly owned subsidiary of Berkshire Hathaway. It began as a savings and loan association, but eventually grew to control Precision Steel Corp., CORT Furniture Leasing, Kansas Bankers Surety Company, and other ventures. Wesco Financial also held a concentrated equity portfolio of over US$1.5 billion in companies such as Coca-Cola, Wells Fargo, Procter & Gamble, Kraft Foods, US Bancorp, and Goldman Sachs. Munger believes that holding a concentrated number of stocks, that he knows extremely well, will in the long term produce superior returns.

Wesco is based in Pasadena, California, Munger's adopted hometown. Pasadena was also the site of the company's annual shareholders' meeting, which were typically held on the Wednesday or Thursday after the more famous Berkshire Hathaway annual meeting. Munger's meetings were nearly as legendary in the investment community as those he co-hosts with Buffett in Omaha. Such meetings were often perfunctory, but Munger interacted with the other Wesco shareholders at considerable length, sometimes speculating about what Benjamin Franklin would do in a given situation. Meeting notes have been posted on the Futile Finance? website, but no updates exist beyond 2011.

Munger is also the chairman of Daily Journal Corporation. Since Wesco meetings ended, the Daily Journal annual meeting has grown in importance, as investors flock to the meeting to listen to him speak at length.

Blueprint

Develop a healthy relationship with the truth.

"I think that one should recognize reality even when one doesn't like it; indeed, especially when one doesn't like it." -- Munger

As an entrepreneur, it's surprisingly easy to develop tunnel vision -- keeping your eyes glued to the prize. As a result, you can grow ignorant to the ugly facts and truths surrounding you. A huge aspect of running a business is being able to face harsh realities and fight through them.

Always maintain the student mindset.

"Go to bed smarter than when you woke up." -- Munger

One of the things I like most about Munger is his mindset that one should never stop learning. Ultimately, it doesn't matter who you are or what you've done, no one has all the answers. However, the ones who commit to a lifetime of learning have way more than those who don't.

I firmly believe that every single day is an opportunity to become smarter and more aware of the world around you. As the business world is constantly changing and evolving, this is an especially important mindset to have as an entrepreneur. Otherwise, growth is simply not possible.

The Business

Evaluating the business in which you decide to invest is itself also quite important. Ask yourself if you're investing in a commodity business with no inherent competitive advantage (e.g., a farmer selling apples) – in which case its survival may be harder to determine – or a robust business with a durable competitive advantage.

Certain businesses are able to exploit the benefits of living in a (mostly) market-based society more than others. For example, Costco has thrived in discount retail despite massive competition. Neither Walmart nor Amazon have been able to fully knock Costco off its pedestal. The company's inherent business model allows for growth with increasingly more efficient systems that go on to benefit customers. The resulting sales and margin growth increases Costco's cash flow over time. This excess cash (or at least the proportion attributable to the investor) is ultimately the return on the investors' original investment.

Mental Models

Inversion

All I want to know is where I'm going to die, so I'll never go there. – Charlie Munger

The mental model of inversion comes from a German mathematician, Carl Gustav Jacobi. Jacobi, who worked on elliptic functions, urged his students to "invert, always invert." He thought it was easier to solve difficult problems by looking at them backwards.

According to Munger, many problems can't be solved "forward" – identifying the ideal outcome and taking steps to achieve it.

Instead, he urges us to think about the things we want to avoid happening. What would cause those negative outcomes? How can you avoid them?

Inversion removes a ton of pressure to run your business "perfectly." It also acts as a filter to avoid stupid decisions. It's easier to not be stupid than force yourself to be brilliant every day. With time, avoiding serious mistakes leads you exactly where you want to go: towards success.

Good morals and a reputation

In one of his most recent interviews in April 2019 with the Wall Street Journal, Munger tried to emphasize this point. According to an edited transcript of the interview published in the Journal, when asked about the importance of benefiting from lessons paid for by others, Munger responded:

"I want to learn as much as I can vicariously. It's too painful to do it by personal hardship. Of course. I collect big calamities in my head and big stupidities. I do that so I can avoid them. Think of how little in the way of big calamity has ever come to Berkshire (NYSE:BRK.A) (NYSE:BRK.B). And it's not that we don't ever have reverses and disappointments in that or never have whole businesses disappear. But averaged out, we have less misfortune than others.
Another thing that really helps is people, a lot of people think that real selfishness, very extreme, is what works. But it doesn't...

If you have a reputation for being decent to work with and unselfish, you make more money, not less. And at Berkshire, I can't tell you the things that we have bought where the people wanted a good home for something that they love, and they trusted us to take care of their loved one. That sounds ridiculous to talk about, in that language about businesses. But why wouldn't you love something you spent your life building up? It's very natural to love it – it's your own creation. Of course, you want it in good hands...

Good morals and a reputation for good morals are enormously valuable, and it's just so simple.... The right way to go through life is win-win. Just anything else is crazy. To be all take and no give is just an absolute disaster.

11

Henry Ford

" Whether you think you can, or you think you can't - you're right."

- Henry Ford

Biography

Henry Ford (July 30, 1863 – April 7, 1947) was an American industrialist and business magnate, founder of the Ford Motor Company and chief developer of the assembly line technique of mass production. By creating the first automobile that middle-class Americans could afford, he converted the automobile from an expensive curiosity into an accessible conveyance that would profoundly impact the landscape of the 20th century.

His introduction of the Model T automobile revolutionized transportation and American industry. As the owner of the Ford Motor Company, he became one of the richest and best-known people in the world. He is credited with "Fordism": mass production of inexpensive goods coupled with high wages for workers. Ford had a global vision, with consumerism as the key to peace. His intense commitment to systematically lowering costs resulted in many technical and business innovations, including a franchise system that put dealerships throughout most of North America and in major cities on six continents. Ford left most of his vast wealth to the Ford Foundation and arranged for his family to control the company permanently.

Ford was also widely known for his pacifism during the first years of World War I, and for promoting antisemitic content, including The Protocols of the Elders of Zion, through his newspaper The Dearborn Independent and the book The International Jew, having an alleged influence on the development of Nazism.

Blueprint

Failures are opportunities.

Ford failed many times before he finally succeeded. Such a trajectory is incredibly common among entrepreneurs. Human beings tend to downplay their failures, but the truth is that no person is immune to failure, which is a good thing, since failures are merely opportunities disguised as negative events.

As Ford once said, "Failure is simply the opportunity to begin again, this time more intelligently." In other words, we must take our failures as our teachers.

Naturally, no one likes the experience of failure. It's very disruptive to our sense of optimism and momentum when our plans do not work out. However, we can only benefit from changing the way we tend to think about failure.

"Whether you think you can, or you think you can't — you're right."

It has long been believed that all successes actually begin in the mind. In fact, it is generally accepted that both success and failure occur first in our minds before they present themselves in reality. Henry Ford believed strongly in this principle and lived by it during his daily business life. Most great men and women understand that whatever view you have of yourself in your mind will manifest itself in reality.

So the first objective in any successful venture is to commit mentally to that success — charting a course in your mind that will virtually guarantee positive empirical results.

Have passion for what you do

If you don't have enthusiasm for your work, then it's time to find a new job! While you won't have a perfect work day every day, having a passion for what you do will make everything more worthwhile. It might take some time to find this passion, but Henry Ford's life lessons show us that they are worth fighting for.

Know Your Market

"If I had simply asked people what they wanted, they would have asked me for faster horses!" – Henry Ford

Knowing your target market goes much deeper than simply knowing what they want. Ford believed in offering his customers solutions to problems they didn't even know they had.

Henry Ford knew he was going to build an automobile. Before he built it, though, he conducted extensive research on who would buy it, how much they could afford to pay, and what they would want and need in a car.

By the time the Model T was introduced, Ford already knew he had a large market of potential buyers, what features would make the buy, and what to charge them.

Efficiency Is King

"It has been my observation that most people get ahead during the time that others waste." – Henry Ford

From mass production via the assembly line to economical personal effort, Ford and his company were captains of efficiency.

The assembly line allowed Ford Motor Company to produce automobiles quickly. Ford's treatment of his workers allowed the company to retain employees and produce quality. These two factors combined to create ultimate efficiency.

Focus On Quality

"Quality means doing it right when no one is looking.' – Henry Ford

When you're excited about your product, it can be easy to find yourself in a rush to launch. But to be really passionate involves a lot of due diligence.

Ford insisted that if his name was going to be on the company, the brand would stand for quality. He wanted to be 100% confident in his automobiles before they were sold.

"Don't find fault; find a remedy."

The above is one of my favorite Henry Ford quotes, and it's one of his best life lessons. It's so easy to place blame on other people or to point the finger at someone else for your mistakes. However, one of the most integral skills you can learn in life is taking responsibility for your actions. Even better, take it one step further and find a solution to the problem. This will guarantee you much success in life.

Use Your Time Wisely

"It has been my observation that most people get ahead during the time that others waste."

It can be easy to become distracted with cell phones, social media, and television. We are fed a constant stream of information which distracts us from our goals.

Our time on earth is limited, but the things you can accomplish during your lifetime are not. In order to achieve greatness, you have to use your time wisely and efficiently.

Believe In Yourself

"Whether you think that you can, or that you can't, you are usually right."

If you believe that you can accomplish your goals and dreams, you are more than half way there. To achieve anything in life you must believe in yourself and what you are capable of.

Many people do not even try to accomplish their goals and dreams because they don't believe in themselves they don't believe they are capable of achieving their goals.

Believe in yourself, your capabilities, and your goals. Anything is possible if you believe it!

Nothing Is Difficult

"Nothing is particularly hard if you divide it into small jobs."

When we look at the overall challenges that we face they can seem overwhelming. We tend to overcomplicate things in our minds. However, if you break things down into smaller, more achievable tasks, the overall obstacle suddenly is more achievable.

12

Oprah Winfrey

"You don't become what you want, you become what you believe."

— Oprah Winfrey

Biography

Oprah Gail Winfrey (born Orpah Gail Winfrey; January 29, 1954) is an American media executive, actress, talk show host, television producer, and philanthropist. She is best known for her talk show, The Oprah Winfrey Show, broadcast from Chicago, which was the highest-rated television program of its kind in history and ran in national syndication for 25 years from 1986 to 2011. Dubbed the "Queen of All Media", she was the richest African American of the 20th century and North America's first black multi-billionaire, and she has been ranked the greatest black philanthropist in American history. By 2007, she was sometimes ranked as the most influential woman in the world.

Winfrey was born into poverty in rural Mississippi to a teenage single mother and later raised in inner-city Milwaukee. She has stated that she was molested during her childhood and early teens and became pregnant at 14; her son was born prematurely and died in infancy. Winfrey was then sent to live with the man she calls her father, Vernon Winfrey, a barber in Tennessee, and landed a job in radio while still in high school. By 19, she was a co-anchor for the local evening news. Winfrey's often emotional, extemporaneous delivery eventually led to her transfer to the daytime talk show arena, and after boosting a third-rated local Chicago talk show to first place, she launched her own production company and became internationally syndicated.

Credited with creating a more intimate, confessional form of media communication, Winfrey popularized and revolutionized the tabloid talk show genre pioneered by Phil Donahue. Through this medium, Winfrey broke 20th-century taboos and allowed LGBT people to enter the mainstream through television appearances. In 1994, she was inducted into the National Women's Hall of Fame.

By the mid-1990s, Winfrey had reinvented her show with a focus on literature, self-improvement, mindfulness, and spirituality. Though she was criticized for unleashing a confession culture, promoting controversial self-help ideas,and having an emotion-centered approach, she has also been praised for overcoming adversity to become a benefactor to others. Winfrey had also emerged as a political force in the 2008 presidential race, delivering about one million votes to Barack Obama in the razor close 2008 Democratic primary.In 2013, Winfrey was awarded the Presidential Medal of Freedom by President Obama and honorary doctorate degrees from Duke and Harvard.In 2008, she formed her own network, Oprah Winfrey Network (OWN)

Blueprint

Success takes time

Many entrepreneurs go into business thinking that they have raised enough money to launch the business. But, the foundation of a business doesn't happen overnight. It typically takes two or three years to build a solid foundation and ensure the business is on steady ground.

I use a phrase that I call "TGFO" (Thank God For Oprah), because when she started the Oprah Winfrey Network, it took her just about three years to get her foundation settled. Now, I have that to point to as a benchmark.

Listen to Your Own Voice

Your uniqueness is something competitors can't imitate. Oprah didn't dominate as a talk show host by imitating Phil Donahue — she did so by doing it her way.

In business, success has many different paths. By copying where others are excelling, you're bringing little value to the market and providing no reason for people to choose to do business with you as opposed to someone else. Additionally, focusing too much on the competition takes time and energy away from you. Oprah is quoted as saying:

"You can't control the other guy. You only have control over yourself."

Oprah has competed with over 100 talk shows from Ricki Lake to Geraldo Rivera to Sally Jessy Raphael. She persevered and outperformed all these shows because she focused on providing quality content that she and her viewers wanted to see — and less so on ratings and competition.

Believe and Invest in Yourself

Oprah didn't become a communications mogul who inspires millions by taking the easy route or following a traditional career path. Oprah intentionally and strategically made decisions that would have the greatest benefits for her in the long term.

"The only people who never tumble are those who never mount the high wire."

In 1988, Oprah's talk show went national. At this time, she was faced with a choice: owning the show herself or drawing a salary. On the advice of her attorney, she chose the former and acquired "The Oprah Winfrey Show" from Cap Cities/ABC and founded Harpo Productions, Inc. She now states that this was one of the best decisions of her life — if someone else owned her show, it would have limited her creative freedom and, ultimately, her success. As you probably know, Harpo Productions now includes film, radio, retail, a magazine and a cable network.

Make a plan that you feel passionate about and strive towards it. Don't make choices that give you the immediate reward. Aggressively pursue the path that will lead you to your ultimate end goal.

Do Your Best, Always

Winfrey has often stated that her definition of luck is when preparation meets opportunity. "My philosophy is that not only are you responsible for your life, but doing the best at this moment, puts you in the best place for the next moment," she said.

Follow Your Intuition

In her taped master class, Winfrey tried to compress the most important lessons she's learned in her life into a couple of hours, and among the great advice she gave in that talk was this gem: "You cannot hear the still, small voice of your instinct, your intuition, what some people call God, if you allow the noise of the world to drown it out," she said. "So, shut out the haters and the well-wishers and the sales clerk who thinks that dress is "so versatile."

Practice Gratitude

The billionaire has preached gratitude as a foundation of living in countless interviews, and most every episode of her talk show has some iteration of this quote, "Be thankful for what you have; you'll end up having more. If you concentrate on what you don't have, you will never, ever have enough."

Never give up hope

Oprah Winfrey accepted a lifetime achievement award at the 2018 Golden Globes, delivering a rousing and moving speech that inspired a standing ovation.

One of the many important things she spoke about was the value of resilience, and of hope.

"I've interviewed and portrayed people who've withstood some of the ugliest things life can throw at you," she said. "But the one quality all of them seem to share is an ability to maintain hope for a brighter morning, even during our darkest nights. So I want all the girls watching here, now, to know that a new day is on the horizon!"

If you haven't fallen, you haven't walked

Oprah, like mostly insanely successful people, doesn't believe in failure.

What most people think of as failure, Winfrey considers to be a new perspective, a new lesson, another stepping stone to her destination. This is the advice she has for those afraid to fail: "Do the one thing you think you cannot do. Fail at it. Try again. Do better."

Invest in yourself

You might think after achieving a certain level of success, someone like Ms. Winfrey might no longer focus on self-improvement.

But this wasn't what Brunson witnessed, who saw the entertainment mogul "spend a significant amount of time dedicating resources to self-development."

The takeaway, says Brunson: "The moment you stop investing in yourself is the moment you have written off future dividends in life."Learn to laugh, at yourself

"You can't go more than two minutes in a conversation with Oprah without her smiling and belting out a laugh--typically at her own expense," says Brunson.

Everyone makes mistakes. If you don't take yourself too seriously, you won't fall apart when you make yours. Others will be drawn to your humility, and every stumble becomes another chance to learn.

Focus on Helping Others

Far too many businesses are only in it for themselves and are not really interested in helping others or satisfying any of their needs. Oprah set out to help others as well as build a profitable business for herself, and by setting out to help others, she benefited herself.

"You know you are on the road to success if you would do your job, and not be paid for it." – Oprah Winfrey

Don't launch a company unless you can give it your full attention.

For many aspiring entrepreneurs, maintaining their regular full-time job while building the company is the only feasible way to achieve their dreams. However, Oprah has publicly warned against moonlighting at your start-up while still working your day job, as it can pose a risk to the ultimate success of your business.

In an interview with Entertainment Weekly, the media mogul expressed regret over her decision to launch her television network OWN before ending her run as the host of her long-running talk show, The Oprah Winfrey Show. In the interview, she alluded to the fact that splitting her time and attention between jobs prevented her from giving her full effort to her new venture.

Just because you're struggling doesn't mean you're failing.

Though today she is frequently featured on Fortune's Most Powerful Women in Business list, Oprah did not find immediate success early on. After working hard to earn her way into a position as a daytime co-anchor for WJZ-TV in Baltimore, Maryland, she was fired and told that she was "unfit for television news." Even after she had found massive success with The Oprah Winfrey Show, she continued to take entrepreneurial risks and navigate disappointments, including the failure of the 1998 film Beloved, in which she held the starring role.

13

Jeff Bezos

Biography

Jeffrey Preston Bezos; born January 12, 1964 is an American industrialist, media proprietor, and investor. He is best known as the founder, CEO, and president of the online retail company Amazon. The first centi-billionaire on the Forbes wealth index, Bezos has been the world's richest person since 2017 and was named the "richest man in modern history" after his net worth increased to $150 billion in July 2018.In September 2018, Forbes described him as "far richer than anyone else on the planet" as he added $1.8 billion to his net worth when Amazon became the second company in history to reach a market cap of $1 trillion.

Born in Albuquerque and raised in Houston and later Miami, Bezos graduated from Princeton University in 1986 with a degree in electrical engineering and computer science. He worked on Wall Street in a variety of related fields from 1986 to early 1994. He founded Amazon in late 1994 on a cross-country road trip from New York City to Seattle. The company began as an online bookstore and has since expanded to a wide variety of other e-commerce products and services, including video and audio streaming, cloud computing, and AI. It is currently the world's largest online sales company, the largest Internet company by revenue, and the world's largest provider of virtual assistants and cloud infrastructure services through its Amazon Web Services branch.

Bezos founded the aerospace manufacturer and sub-orbital spaceflight services company Blue Origin in 2000. A Blue Origin test flight successfully first reached space in 2015, and the company has upcoming plans to begin commercial suborbital human spaceflight. He also purchased the major American newspaper The Washington Post in 2013 for $250 million in cash, and manages many other investments through his Bezos Expeditions venture capital firm.

Blueprint

Be Stubborn and Flexible

According to Bezos, good entrepreneurs must be stubborn and flexible. When referring to Amazon, Bezos says, "We are stubborn on vision. We are flexible on details."

Sticking to the vision is the first part, and being flexible about the tactics is the second part. Bezos adds, "If you're not stubborn, you'll give up on experiments too soon. And if you're not flexible, you'll pound your head against the wall and you won't see a different solution to a problem you're trying to solve."

There's a challenge in being stubborn and flexible. Bezos warns: "The thing about inventing is you have to be both stubborn and flexible, more or less simultaneously. The hard part is figuring out when to be which!"

Never Stop Experimenting

"If you double the number of experiments you do per year you're going to double your inventiveness."

If you ask most CEOs, they'll tell you that experimentation is imperative for their business. It's how new innovations are born and how they stay competitive in the market. Automotive companies have concept cars; food companies experiment with new foods and flavors; retail companies experiment with placement of products and store atmosphere; drug companies are built on experimentation; tech companies have "labs" like Google Labs; and many high performing companies, like Google, allow their employees to experiment. Even sports teams experiment with new plays and/or players. Experimentation is everywhere and is always happening.

At Amazon, experimentation and willingness to invent has always been a part of the culture. It's not secondary or something that "has to be done because everyone else does it."

How to make money?

Many people are confused about Amazon — they think that Amazon's value is by selling things. Instead, the strength of Amazon is the recommendation engine, as well as the system of reviews on products. Jeff Bezos says the following:

"We don't make money when we sell things. We make money when we help customers make purchasing decisions".

In today's world, there are billions of ways to add value to the lives of others. To help others make decisions is a huge field that is still largely untapped.

The customer always comes first

One of the things which has helped Amazon become so successful is Jeff Bezos' belief in always serving the customer first.

He knew that customers wanted low prices, faster shipping — so he made that a priority of the company (which prevented Amazon from turning a profit).

Yet Bezos is in the long-run game with Amazon. He knew that if you did everything to please the customer, he would get customers hooked (like myself), and then build long-term value.

Minimize Regret

When Bezos was debating whether or not to quit his day job and start Amazon.com, he realized that he lacked an analytical framework for making big life decisions. So he made one up:

"The framework I found which made the decision incredibly easy was what I called – which only a nerd would call – a 'regret minimization framework'. So I wanted to project myself forward to age 80 and say, 'Okay, now I'm looking back on my life. I want to have minimized the number of regrets I have.'"

In this big-picture perspective, the right decision was clear. He wouldn't regret losing his job at the age of 80 (surely he would have found another good job by then), but he would still be kicking himself for not cashing in on the online gold rush (at that time, the Internet was growing at a rate of 2300% per year).

"I knew that if I failed I wouldn't regret that, but I knew the one thing I might regret is not trying."

Give Bezos' "regret minimization framework" a shot for yourself. You may be surprised what action it inspires you to take.

Encourage Word of Mouth

When Bezos started Amazon he didn't have a marketing budget. The only way his company would succeed was if it was so good that it spread by word of mouth.

"If you build a great experience, customers tell each other about that. Word of mouth is very powerful."

There's no better way for a business to grow than through positive word of mouth. The only way to achieve that is to deliver a product or service that's worth talking about. Part of that means providing excellent customer service...

Be Realistic

One of my favorite quotes is from Will Smith: "Being realistic is the most commonly traveled road to mediocrity." The idea is that if you never allow yourself to imagine an extraordinary life, there's no way you'll ever obtain one.

On the other hand, it's possible to dream a little bit too wildly – and I think this affliction is particularly common with entrepreneurs. If you expect overnight success with minimal effort, you're setting yourself up for never-ending frustration and disappointment.

As Bezos points out, being realistic about your business is also a way to ease the pressure of being an entrepreneur:

"It's very important for entrepreneurs to be realistic. So if you believe on that first day while you're writing the business plan that there's a 70 percent chance that the whole thing will fail, then that kind of relieves the pressure of self-doubt."

14

Bill Gates

Biography

William Henry Gates III (born October 28, 1955) is an American business magnate, software developer, investor, and philanthropist. He is best known as the co-founder of Microsoft Corporation. During his career at Microsoft, Gates held the positions of chairman, chief executive officer (CEO), president and chief software architect, while also being the largest individual shareholder until May 2014. He is one of the best-known entrepreneurs and pioneers of the microcomputer revolution of the 1970s and 1980s.

Born and raised in Seattle, Washington, Gates co-founded Microsoft with childhood friend Paul Allen in 1975, in Albuquerque, New Mexico; it went on to become the world's largest personal computer software company. Gates led the company as chairman and CEO until stepping down as CEO in January 2000, but he remained chairman and became chief software architect. During the late 1990s, Gates had been criticized for his business tactics, which have been considered anti-competitive. This opinion has been upheld by numerous court rulings. In June 2006, Gates announced that he would be transitioning to a part-time role at Microsoft and full-time work at the Bill & Melinda Gates Foundation, the private charitable foundation that he and his wife, Melinda Gates, established in 2000. He gradually transferred his duties to Ray Ozzie and Craig Mundie. He stepped down as chairman of Microsoft in February 2014 and assumed a new post as technology adviser to support the newly appointed CEO Satya Nadella.

Since 1987, he has been included in the Forbes list of the world's wealthiest people. From 1995 to 2017, he held the Forbes title of the richest person in the world all but four of those years. In October 2017, he was surpassed by Amazon founder and CEO Jeff Bezos, who had an estimated net worth of US$90.6 billion compared to Gates' net worth of US$89.9 billion at the time.[14] As of November 2019, Gates had an estimated net worth of US$107.1 billion, making him the second-wealthiest person in the world, behind Bezos.

Later in his career and since leaving day-to-day operations at Microsoft in 2008, Gates pursued a number of philanthropic endeavors. He donated large amounts of money to various charitable organizations and scientific research programs through the Bill & Melinda Gates Foundation, reported to be the world's largest private charity. In 2009, Gates and Warren Buffett founded The Giving Pledge, whereby they and other billionaires pledge to give at least half of their wealth to philanthropy. The foundation says that it works to save lives and improve global health, and is working with Rotary International to eliminate polio.

Blueprint

Start as Early as Possible

The first of Bill Gates' success lessons is to start as early as possible; Bill Gates was only 13 years old when he started working with computers. When you start something at an early point in your life, you become molded around it. Not only will you have a chance of becoming successful sooner than most people, but you would also be less likely to want to give up.

If you've had a dream that you start working towards when you're young, you will be more immune to people telling you what you can or can't do.

By the time you're an adult and people actually start to take more notice of what you're working towards, you will be stubborn enough to just ignore them.

Be Your Own Boss as Soon as Possible

Bill Gates became a boss at a fairly early age. He deserved it, and it put him in an excellent position with pure control over his success.

"If you don't build your dream, someone else will hire you to build theirs." – Bill Gates

Don't Whine About Your Mistakes, Learn from Them

What is the pointing in blaming other people for your mistakes? Who are you trying to fool? Your mistakes are on you, they are not anyone else's fault, so stop blaming other people just to try and rid your conscience of guilt.

Mistakes are made to be learnt from. You now know what or what not to do in the same situation when it rolls around for a second time and believe me, in most cases it will roll around again.

"If you mess up, it's not your parents' fault, so don't whine about your mistakes, learn from them." – Bill Gates

Be Committed and Passionate

I think this is always included by every entrepreneur as a good bit of advice. You need to be committed to what you love and have great passion for what you do.

The successful people in this world make it look so easy because they absolutely love what they are doing. If you're finding things too stressful and too hard, then I'm not sure you're working on the right thing.

Life is the Best School, Not University or College

No matter how many books you read, no matter how many tests you take, nothing from university or college can properly prepare you for life in the real world.

Real life jobs and bosses does not just involve you studying and them teaching you. It's real life work that you need to be able to carry out, otherwise you will be fired. End of.

"If you think your teacher is tough, wait until you get a boss. He doesn't have tenure." – Bill Gates

Life is Not Fair

Another of Bill Gates' success lessons is to learn that life is not fair.

No matter how hard you work in life, there will always be times where things don't go your way, perhaps through no fault of your own. Things that you cannot control. You will get knocked down, but you need to be able to stand up.

Life isn't fair. It's a test, a game, a risk. If you fall down and don't bother getting back up, you don't deserve to be successful. Winners know that life isn't fair and they will keep getting back up until they've made it.

"Life is not fair. Get used to it." – Bill Gates

Be Ready to Takes Risks

Starting a business is a little bit like gambling, you're not always sure if you'll win or not. However, the only difference is that you can strategize and plan well enough to ensure the success of your business.

This quote from Bill Gates is not only applicable to entrepreneurs, it can also apply in life as a whole. The world is full of uncertainties. Life has no rules and you have to sacrifice certain things to get to your destination.

People will step on and reject you but at the end of the day, if you are able to muster the courage to keep on going, nothing will stand in your way.

"Business is a money game with few rules and a lot of risk." – Bill Gates

Your Time Is Valuable

Bill Gates always teaches young entrepreneurs the value of time so that they refrain from whiling away their precious work hours. That is why he advises entrepreneurs to pick their battles carefully. Even the richest men in the world cannot buy time as one of his quotes suggests,

"No matter how much money you have, you can't buy more time."

Never Give Up

No matter how difficult the circumstances seem, you should have a "never say die" attitude if you want to succeed. Failure is part of entrepreneurial life and it even affected the greatest entrepreneur in the world. Before the inception of Microsoft, Bill Gates and Paul Allen started Traf-O-Data, a company responsible for analyzing traffic data. Unfortunately, it failed miserably and left Gates under a lot of debt.

He learned important lessons from this failure and moved on to launch Microsoft. Even with Microsoft, he faced initial failure but his unflinching attitude helped him dredge on. Finally, success knocked at his door and he got the reward for not giving up on his dreams.

Focus on Unhappy Customers

Most entrepreneurs treat their disgruntled customers rudely. They think that they are right in doing so but the greatest visionary of our time has a different opinion. He considers dissatisfied customers a huge asset since they can impart lessons you hitherto didn't know. He said, "Your most unhappy customers are your greatest source of learning". If you want to be successful in business, you should listen and value what your disappointed customers are saying. Take action and improve in the light of their feedback.

Innovation is the heart and soul of a business

It's about bringing ideas to market and applying research. If you don't innovate you die. The world keeps changing.

To stay ahead of the game, or even to stay in the game, you have to keep innovating: innovate in your products, innovate in your process, innovate in the markets, etc.

Bill Gates uses innovation as a way to drive impact whether it's shaping software or saving the planet.

15

Thomas Edison

Many of **Life's Failures** are people who do not realise how close they were **to Success** when they **GaveUp**

-*Thomas Edison*

Biography

Thomas Alva Edison (February 11, 1847 – October 18, 1931) was an American inventor and businessman who has been described as America's greatest inventor. He developed many devices in fields such as electric power generation, mass communication, sound recording, and motion pictures. These inventions, which include the phonograph, the motion picture camera, and the long-lasting, practical electric light bulb, have had a widespread impact on the modern industrialized world. He was one of the first inventors to apply the principles of organized science and teamwork to the process of invention, working with many researchers and employees. He established the first industrial research laboratory.

Edison was raised in the American Midwest; early in his career he worked as a telegraph operator, which inspired some of his earliest inventions. In 1876, he established his first laboratory facility in Menlo Park, New Jersey, where many of his early inventions were developed. He later established a botanic laboratory in Fort Myers, Florida in collaboration with businessmen Henry Ford and Harvey Firestone, and a laboratory in West Orange, New Jersey that featured the world's first film studio, the Black Maria. He was a prolific inventor, holding 1,093 US patents in his name, as well as patents in other countries. Edison married twice and fathered six children. He died in 1931 of complications of diabetes.

Blueprint

Impossibility

"Nearly every man who develops an idea works it up to the point where it looks impossible, and then he gets discouraged. That's not the place to become discouraged."

Roadblocks are sign-posts letting you know that success is just around the corner. They are there to keep the uncommitted out.

Don't get discouraged when things seem impossible. Remember that it's darkest just before dawn.

Perspiration

"Genius is one percent inspiration and ninety-nine percent perspiration."

Thomas Edison said: "The reason a lot of people do not recognize opportunity is because it goes around wearing overalls and it looks like hard work."

Capability

"If we did all the things we are capable of, we would literally astound ourselves."

Most people are living considerably beneath their capabilities. They've never focused all of their efforts on a singular task.

This is why they are completely unaware of the power they possess. Everyone is good at something, and if singular focus is given to that talent over the course of years, amazing things will be done. You are capable of astonishing yourself!

Restlessness

"Restlessness is discontent and discontent is the first necessity of progress."

Thomas Edison said, "Show me a thoroughly satisfied man and I will show you a failure."

As long as you're perfectly content, you can't make progress. Nothing happens until you become discontented.

If you can live with being 30 pounds over weight, then you won't have the power to change it. Remember, "discontent is the first necessity of progress".

Perspective

"I have not failed. I've just found 10,000 ways that won't work."

Edison said, "Results! Why, man, I have gotten a lot of results. I know several thousand things that won't work."

That's the way we should view our life not as a compilation of failures, but as series of necessary experiments letting us know what doesn't work. From this perspective, we can move into doing what works and from there, we can succeed.

Hard work, Stick-to-itiveness, and Common Sense

"The three great essentials to achieve anything worthwhile are: Hard work, Stick-to-itiveness, and Common sense."

Nothing can replace hard work as its fundamental to success. If you're not willing to work hard, you won't even have a chance at success. No one succeeds and says "That was really easy!"

How Thomas Edison mother's Letter turned him into Genius

"If you learn from your mistakes then you are intelligent. But if you learn from someone's mistakes, then you are a Genius.

One day, as a little boy, Thomas Edison got back home from school and gave paper to his mom. He said to her, Mother my teacher gave this paper to me and revealed to me just you are to peruse it. What does it say? Her eyes filled with tears, she read the letter anyone can hear about her boy.

"Your son is a Genius. This school is not the right place for him, and there are no efficient teachers to train him. So, please train him yourself."

Edison went to School only for 3 months. It was turning point for him because; he explored many things and developed interest in physics and mathematics.

Many years later after Edison's mother passed away, Thomas Alva Edison had become one of the Greatest inventors of the Century. One day, he was checking his cupboard and found a letter, and it was that his childhood teacher wrote to his mother that day. Edison opened the letter.

The matter written in the letter was, " School cannot allow your son to attend classes anymore, he is mentally impaired. He is rusticated."

Edison became emotional reading it and then wrote in his diary... *"Thomas A. Edison was a mentally deficient child, whose mother turned him into The Genius of the century."*

A positive word of Encouragement can help change anyone's destiny.

16

J.K. Rowling

Biography

Joanne Rowling (born 31 July 1965), better known by her pen name J. K. Rowling, is a British author, film producer, television producer, screenwriter, and philanthropist. She is best known for writing the Harry Potter fantasy series, which has won multiple awards and sold more than 500 million copies, becoming the best-selling book series in history.[The books are the basis of a popular film series, over which Rowling had overall approval on the scripts and was a producer on the final films. She also writes crime fiction under the name Robert Galbraith.

Born in Yate, Gloucestershire, Rowling was working as a researcher and bilingual secretary for Amnesty International when she conceived the idea for the Harry Potter series while on a delayed train from Manchester to London in 1990. The seven-year period that followed saw the death of her mother, birth of her first child, divorce from her first husband, and relative poverty until the first novel in the series, Harry Potter and the Philosopher's Stone, was published in 1997. There were six sequels, of which the last, Harry Potter and the Deathly Hallows, was released in 2007. Since then, Rowling has written five books for adult readers: The Casual Vacancy (2012) and—under the pseudonym Robert Galbraith—the crime fiction Cormoran Strike series, which consists of The Cuckoo's Calling (2013), The Silkworm (2014), Career of Evil (2015), and Lethal White (2018).

Rowling has lived a "rags to riches" life in which she progressed from living on benefits to being named the world's first billionaire author by Forbes. However, Rowling disputed the assertion, saying she was not a billionaire.Forbes reported that she lost her billionaire status after giving away much of her earnings to charity but remains one of the wealthiest people in the world. She is the UK's best-selling living author, with sales in excess of £238 million. The 2019 Sunday Times Rich List estimated Rowling's fortune at £750 million, ranking her as the joint 191st richest person in the UK. Time named her a runner-up for its 2007 Person of the Year, noting the social, moral, and political inspiration she has given her fans. In October 2010, Rowling was named the "Most Influential Woman in Britain" by leading magazine editors. She has supported multiple charities, including Comic Relief, One Parent Families, and Multiple Sclerosis Society of Great Britain, as well as launching her own charity, Lumos.

Blueprint

"Rock bottom became the solid foundation on which I rebuilt my life."

"I had failed on an epic scale. An exceptionally short lived marriage had imploded and I was a jobless alone parent and as poor as it was possible to be in Britain without being homeless."

You too can build up from your own rock bottom, laying a foundation for your dreams and goals, no matter where you are at in this very moment.

"Failure gave me an inner security that I have never had by passing examinations."

Does inner security comes from a job, money, getting an A? The perfect spouse or relationship?

Not according to Jo. Her inner security came from failure.

"Failure meant the stripping away of the inessential."

What can you strip away? What is inessential in your life? What will be left? What's left is only what's important to you along with inner security that you are choosing only a path that is right for you.

"Poverty itself is romanticized only by fools. It means a thousand petty humiliations and hardships."

Jo disagrees. Why romanticize humiliation and hardships?

"I cannot criticize my parents for hoping I would never experience poverty. They had been poor themselves and I have since been poor. And I quite agree with them that it is not an ennobling experience."

It may be time for you to romanticize wealth and abundance, and look forward to bringing your gifts to this world, while satiated, with some extra money in the bank. Now that is ennobling.

"The moment you are old enough to take the wheel, responsibility lies with you."

If you're blaming someone else for you not finding your own dream and bringing it to life, grab the wheel; you're old enough to drive.

"I do not blame my parents...there is an expiry date for blaming your parents for steering you in the wrong direction. I discovered that I had a strong will and more discipline than I had suspected."

You have what it takes, so take it. The minute you stop blaming, you can start steering.

"We do not need magic to transform our world. We carry all the power we need inside ourselves already."

Wouldn't it be nice to have Harry or Hermione's magic wand? Or to go into a wand shop and browse?

If Jo tells you that you have magic and power inside yourself, then you do. Believe it, allow it to surface and get ready for a wild ride.

"The crucial importance of imagination."

Did you think imagination is to be left for the kids? Maybe you're just a big kid after all.

"Imagination is not only the uniquely human capacity to envision that which is not and therefore the fount of all invention…we have the power to imagine better."

"It is the power that enables us to empathize with humans whose experiences we never shared."

Go ahead and daydream. Let your imagination run where it may and imagine a better life, a better world. You have Jo's permission.

"I began to direct all my energy into finishing the only work that mattered to me."

What work matters to you?

"I stopped pretending to myself that I was anything other than what I was."

What might you be pretending to be? What box are you in? Climb on out.

"It is impossible to live without failing at something unless you live so cautiously that you might not have lived at all, in which case you fail by default."

Failure is good. It means you are out in the ring, not in the nosebleed section, watching other people battle it out.

"There was a point where I really felt I had 'penniless divorcee lone parent' tattooed on my head."

"What I feared most; failure. I was the biggest failure I knew."

Stay Focused

It took Rowling five years to outline the plots for all the books.

Now, most people don't have five years to work on something. But the key here is to stay focused. Don't let the nonessentials make you lose focus.

Bloomsbury, the small publisher that published Rowling's first book, suggested she get a day job "since she had little chance of making money in children's books."

It's a good thing she kept her eye on the prize, and didn't let that discourage her – each Harry Potter book broke sales records.

Don't Give Up

This goes hand-in-hand with the previous lesson. Once you have a great idea, don't give up on it.

Rowling was rejected by 12 publishing houses, but she never gave up.

Life and work are full of challenges. Don't let them derail you. Find a way to make it work and persevere.

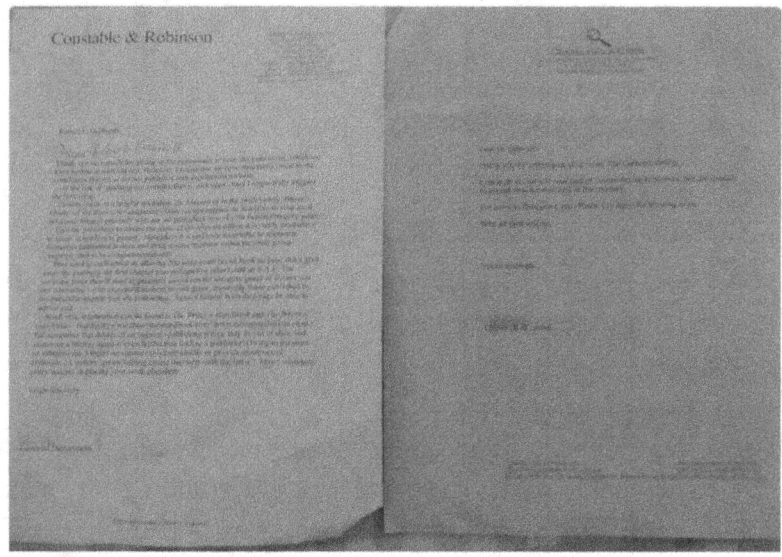

 J.K. Rowling
@jk_rowling

 Follow

By popular request, 2 of @RGalbrath's rejection letters! (For inspiration, not revenge, so I've removed signatures.)
9:37 AM - 25 Mar 2016

 4,430   11,950

Don't Second Guess Your Great Ideas

If you have an idea you feel passionate about, go for it. Don't rationalize it and second-guess it to death. That's how you talk yourself out of something.

If you feel that much passion over an idea, you need to follow through with it.

Be Patient

After Rowling finished her book, it took a year to get it published.

Don't try to rush things. When people rush, mistakes are made. Take your time, remain calm and prepared for the next step.

Learn To Accept Criticism

No matter what you do, someone will always have something negative to say about it. Don't let that stop you or deter you.

Not only was Rowling's book rejected numerous times, but to this day some schools won't allow the series in their libraries because they are about witchcraft and wizardry.
"Failure meant a stripping away of the inessential. I stopped pretending to myself that I was anything other than I was and began diverting all my energy into finishing the only work that mattered to me."

17

Sam Walton

> I probably have traveled and walked into more variety stores than anybody in America. I am just trying to get ideas, any kind of ideas that will help our company. Most of us don't invent ideas. We take the best ideas from someone else.
>
> (Sam Walton)

Biography

Samuel Moore Walton (March 29, 1918 – April 5, 1992) was an American businessman and entrepreneur best known for founding the retailers Walmart and Sam's Club. Wal-Mart Stores Inc. grew to be the world's largest corporation by revenue as well as the biggest private employer in the world. For a period of time, Walton was the richest man in America.

In 1945, after leaving the military, Walton took over management of his first variety store at the age of 26. With the help of a $20,000 loan from his father-in-law, plus $5,000 he had saved from his time in the Army, Walton purchased a Ben Franklin variety store in Newport, Arkansas. The store was a franchise of the Butler Brothers chain.

Walton pioneered many concepts that became crucial to his success. According to Walton, if he offered prices as good or better than stores in cities that were four hours away by car, people would shop at home. Walton made sure the shelves were consistently stocked with a wide range of goods. His second store, the tiny "Eagle" department store, was down the street from his first Ben Franklin and next door to its main competitor in Newport.

With the sales volume growing from $80,000 to $225,000 in three years, Walton drew the attention of the landlord, P. K. Holmes, whose family had a history in retail. Admiring Sam's great success, and desiring to reclaim the store (and franchise rights) for his son he refused to renew the lease. The lack of a renewal option, together with the prohibitively high rent of 5% of sales, were early business lessons to Walton. Despite forcing Walton out, Holmes bought the store's inventory and fixtures for $50,000, which Walton called "a fair price".

Walton's Five and Dime, now the Walmart Visitors Center, Bentonville.
With a year left on the lease, but the store effectively sold, he, his wife Helen and his father-in-law managed to negotiate the purchase of a new location on the downtown square of Bentonville, Arkansas. Walton negotiated the purchase of a small discount store, and the title to the building, on the condition that he get a 99-year lease to expand into the shop next door. The owner of the shop next door refused six times, and Walton gave up on Bentonville when his father-in-law, without Sam's knowledge, paid the shop owner a final visit and $20,000 to secure the lease. He had just enough left from the sale of the first store to close the deal, and reimburse Helen's father. They opened for business with a one-day remodeling sale on May 9, 1950.

Before he bought the Bentonville store, it was doing $72,000 in sales and it increased to $105,000 in the first year and then $140,000 and $175,000.

Blueprint

Rule 1: Commit to your business.

Believe in it more than anybody else. I think I overcame every single one of my personal shortcomings by the sheer passion I brought to my work. I don't know if you're born with this kind of passion, or if you can learn it. But I do know you need it. If you love your work, you'll be out there every day trying to do it the best you possibly can, and pretty soon everybody around will catch the passion from you — like a fever.

Rule 2: Share your profits with all your associates, and treat them as partners.

In turn, they will treat you as a partner, and together you will all perform beyond your wildest expectations. Remain a corporation and retain control if you like, but behave as a servant leader in your partnership. Encourage your associates to hold a stake in the company. Offer discounted stock, and grant them stock for their retirement. It's the single best thing we ever did.

Rule 3: Motivate your partners.

Money and ownership alone aren't enough. Constantly, day by day, think of new and more interesting ways to motivate and challenge your partners. Set high goals, encourage competition, and then keep score. Make bets with outrageous payoffs. If things get stale, cross-pollinate; have managers switch jobs with one another to stay challenged. Keep everybody guessing as to what your next trick is going to be. Don't become too predictable.

Rule 4: Communicate everything you possibly can to your partners.

The more they know, the more they'll understand. The more they understand, the more they'll care. Once they care, there's no stopping them. If you don't trust your associates to know what's going on, they'll know you really don't consider them partners. Information is power, and the gain you get from empowering your associates more than offsets the risk of informing your competitors.

Rule 5: Appreciate everything your associates do for the business.

A paycheck and a stock option will buy one kind of loyalty. But all of us like to be told how much somebody appreciates what we do for them. We like to hear it often, and especially when we have done something we're really proud of. Nothing else can quite substitute for a few well-chosen, well-timed, sincere words of praise. They're absolutely free — and worth a fortune.

Rule 6: Celebrate your success.

Find some humor in your failures. Don't take yourself so seriously. Loosen up, and everybody around you will loosen up. Have fun. Show enthusiasm — always. When all else fails, put on a costume and sing a silly song. Then make everybody else sing with you. Don't do a hula on Wall Street. It's been done. Think up your own stunt. All of this is more important, and more fun, than you think, and it really fools competition. "Why should we take those cornballs at Wal-Mart seriously?"

Rule 7: Listen to everyone in your company and figure out ways to get them talking.

The folks on the front lines — the ones who actually talk to the customer — are the only ones who really know what's going on out there. You'd better find out what they know. This really is what total quality is all about. To push responsibility down in your organization, and to force good ideas to bubble up within it, you must listen to what your associates are trying to tell you.

Rule 8: Exceed your customer's expectations.

If you do, they'll come back over and over. Give them what they want — and a little more. Let them know you appreciate them. Make good on all your mistakes, and don't make excuses — apologize. Stand behind everything you do. The two most important words I ever wrote were on that first Wal-Mart sign: "Satisfaction Guaranteed." They're still up there, and they have made all the difference.

Rule 9: Control your expenses better than your competition.

This is where you can always find the competitive advantage. For twenty-five years running — long before Wal-Mart was known as the nation's largest retailer — we've ranked No. 1

in our industry for the lowest ratio of expenses to sales. You can make a lot of different mistakes and still recover if you run an efficient operation. Or you can be brilliant and still go out of business if you're too inefficient.

Rule 10: Swim upstream.

Go the other way. Ignore the conventional wisdom. If everybody else is doing it one way, there's a good chance you can find your niche by going in exactly the opposite direction. But be prepared for a lot of folks to wave you down and tell you you're headed the wrong way. I guess in all my years, what I heard more often than anything was: a town of less than 50,000 population cannot support a discount store for very long.

18

Arnold Schwarzenegger

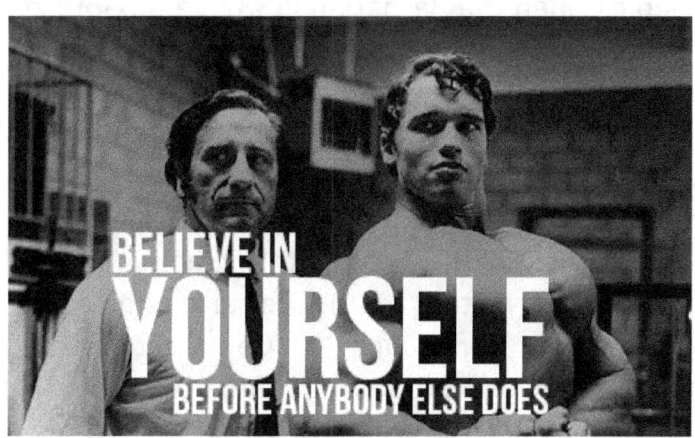

Biography

Arnold Alois Schwarzenegger (born July 30, 1947) is an Austrian-American actor, filmmaker, businessman, author, and former politician and professional bodybuilder.[He served as the 38th Governor of California from 2003 to 2011. As of 2020, he is the most recent Republican governor of California.

Schwarzenegger began lifting weights at the age of 15, and went on to win the Mr. Universe title at age 20 before winning the Mr. Olympia contest seven times; he remains a prominent presence in bodybuilding and has written many books and articles on the sport. The Arnold Sports Festival, considered the second most important bodybuilding event after Mr. Olympia,is named after him. He is widely regarded as one of the greatest bodybuilders of all time, as well as the sport's most charismatic and famous ambassador.

Schwarzenegger gained worldwide fame as a Hollywood action film icon. His breakthrough film was the sword-and-sorcery epic Conan the Barbarian (1982), a box-office hit that resulted in a sequel in 1984. He appeared as the title character in James Cameron's critically and commercially successful sci-fi action film The Terminator (1984), and subsequently played a similar character in the films Terminator 2: Judgment Day (1991), Terminator 3: Rise of the Machines (2003), Terminator Genisys (2015), and Terminator: Dark Fate (2019). He also starred in other successful action films such as Commando (1985), The Running Man (1987), Predator (1987), Total Recall (1990), and True Lies (1994), in addition to comedy films such as Twins (1988), Kindergarten Cop (1990), Junior (1994), and Jingle All The Way (1996).

A Republican, Schwarzenegger was first elected on October 7, 2003, in a special recall election to replace then-Governor Gray Davis. He was sworn in on November 17, to serve the remainder of Davis' term. He was then re-elected in the 2006 California gubernatorial election, to serve a full term as governor. In 2011, he completed his second term as governor and returned to acting.

Schwarzenegger is considered among the most important figures in the history of bodybuilding, and his legacy is commemorated in the Arnold Classic annual bodybuilding competition. He has remained a prominent face in bodybuilding long after his retirement, in part because of his ownership of gyms and fitness magazines. He has presided over numerous contests and awards shows.

For many years, he wrote a monthly column for the bodybuilding magazines Muscle & Fitness and Flex. Shortly after being elected governor, he was appointed the executive editor of both magazines, in a largely symbolic capacity. The magazines agreed to donate $250,000 a year to the Governor's various physical fitness initiatives. When the deal, including the contract that gave Schwarzenegger at least $1 million a year, was made public in 2005, many criticized it as being a conflict of interest since the governor's office made decisions concerning regulation of dietary supplements in California. Consequently, Schwarzenegger relinquished the executive editor role in 2005. American Media Inc., which owns Muscle & Fitness and Flex, announced in March 2013 that Schwarzenegger had accepted their renewed offer to be executive editor of the magazines.

One of the first competitions he won was the Junior Mr. Europe contest in 1965.[8] He won Mr. Europe the following year, at age 19. He would go on to compete in many bodybuilding contests, and win most of them. His bodybuilding victories included five Mr. Universe wins (4 – NABBA [England], 1 – IFBB [USA]), and seven Mr. Olympia wins, a record which would stand until Lee Haney won his eighth consecutive Mr. Olympia title in 1991.

Schwarzenegger continues to work out. When asked about his personal training during the 2011 Arnold Classic he said that he was still working out a half an hour with weights every day.

Blueprint

Define Your Goals

Success means different things to different people. Some people define it by money, others by achievement and recognition, others still by experiences or freedom to accrue them.

Whatever the case, it's important to know what success means to you and how to define or quantify it so that you're not stumbling aimlessly. Before you can reach a goal, you must first know what it is.

Enjoy the Process

The journey to success — however you define it — is usually a long one. Now, I'll be the first to say that I think goals are extremely important, and there is great satisfaction in achieving them, but if the only happiness you get is from accomplishing your task, then chances are you aren't going to be happy that often.

Arnold certainly knew this. Obviously, the man thrived on success and worked his ass off to win championships, but he also enjoyed the journey. Arnold found ways to enjoy the process of transforming his body into a championship physique.

You Are Who You Surround Yourself With

This is a concept that nearly everyone in business tends to understand naturally. To put things more quantifiably, the thought is more often expressed as, "you are the average of the five people you spend the most time with."

Forget competing

Losing to Chet Yorton in a bodybuilding competition taught Arnold a valuable lesson. It taught him that you must go into a battle to win and not to compete. Arnold would often visualise himself winning a competition, and his thoughts were full of nothing other than a clear focus to achieve his goal. Nothing was going to stop him from being the best, and he insisted on aiming high.

Staying on top of the hill is harder than climbing it

Once Arnold reached the top in bodybuilding, he found himself at one point where he got lazy, complacent and distracted by study because he had already achieved his big goal. For him, it was harder to stay on top of the hill than climb it.

Having an enormous hill to climb to reach your dreams gives you motivation, but once you achieve your dream, it's much harder to sustain the success long term because the motivation is now gone. Using lessons from Arnold's life, you always need to have a goal that motivates you and is different than your previous pursuits. This is how you stay on top of the hill.

"Every rep and every set is getting me closer to my goal" – Arnold Schwarzenegger

The whole world is not focused on your failure

Arnold's movie "Last Action Hero" was a flop and in the book he described what that's like. He says, "You tend to assume that the whole world is focused on your failure."

Upon reflection, Arnold realises that most of the time people have no idea of your failures nor do they care. They're probably not reading up in detail about you online or watching YouTube video's 24/7 about you. This is an illusion we have, and people have their own problems to worry about.

Your failure will consume you if you spend every waking minute thinking about how people are reacting to your pitfalls in life. Instead, focus on your next win and don't dwell on the past.

Think Big

Never ever settle for anything small. Always think big. This is what Arnold always has believed in firmly. Despite people ridiculing him, he never stopped dreaming big.

If I can see it and believe it, then I can achieve it.

You achieve big things only when you dream & do big things.

19

Jack Ma

Biography

Jack Ma, or Ma Yunborn 10 September 1964), is a Chinese business magnate, investor and politician. He is the co-founder and former executive chairman of Alibaba Group, a multinational technology conglomerate. Ma is a strong proponent of an open and market-driven economy.

Ma is a global ambassador for Chinese business and is often listed as one of the world's most powerful people, with Forbes ranking him 21st on its "World's Most Powerful People" list. He also serves as a role model for startup businesses. In 2017, Ma was ranked second in the annual "World's 50 Greatest Leaders" list by Fortune. In September 2018, he announced that he would retire from Alibaba and pursue educational work, philanthropy, and environmental causes; the following year, Daniel Zhang succeeded him as executive chairman.

As of April 2020, Ma is the second-wealthiest person in China, with a net worth of $42.1 billion, as well as one of the wealthiest people in the world, ranked 17th by Forbes. In 2019, Forbes named Ma in its list of "Asia's 2019 Heroes of Philanthropy" for his work supporting underprivileged communities in China, Africa, Australia, and the Middle East,

Ma applied for 30 different jobs and got rejected by all. "I went for a job with the police; they said, 'you're no good'", Ma told interviewer Charlie Rose. "I even went to KFC when it came to my city. Twenty-four people went for the job. Twenty-three were accepted. I was the only guy ...".

In 1994, Ma heard about the Internet and also started his first company, Hangzhou Haibo Translation Agency. In early 1995, he went to the US with his friends, who helped introduce him to the Internet. Although he found information related to beer from many countries, he was surprised to find none from China. He also tried to search for general information about China and again was surprised to find none. So he and his friend created an "ugly" website related to China. He launched the website at 9:40 AM, and by 12:30 PM he had received emails from some Chinese investors wishing to know about him. This was when Ma realized that the Internet had something great to offer. In April 1995, Ma and He Yibing (a computer teacher) opened the first office for China Pages, and Ma started their second company. On May 10, 1995, they registered the domain chinapages.com in the United States. Within three years, the company had made 5,000,000 Chinese yuan which at the time was equivalent to US$800,000.

Ma began building websites for Chinese companies with the help of friends in the US. He said that "The day we got connected to the Web, I invited friends and TV people over to my house", and on a very slow dial-up connection, "we waited three and a half hours and got half a page", he recalled. "We drank, watched TV and played cards, waiting. But I was so proud. I proved the Internet existed". At a conference in 2010, Ma revealed that he has never actually written a line of code nor made one sale to a customer. He acquired a computer for the first time at the age of 33.

From 1998 to 1999, Ma headed an information technology company established by the China International Electronic Commerce Center, a department of the Ministry of Foreign Trade and Economic Cooperation. In 1999, he quit and returned to Hangzhou with his team to found Alibaba, a China-based business-to-business marketplace site in his apartment with a group of 18 friends. He started a new round of venture development with 500,000 yuan.

Blueprint

Look on the bright side

It's true the economic environment isn't perfect at the moment, but that can be turned to your advantage. All it takes is a simple change of perspective. "If the economic outlook is not perfect, then you will have good competition," he said. "So there are two sides of everything. When everything is fine, then you will have a mediocre company, but when you have headwinds and if a company can live, then this is a great company".

Build a great team

When he founded Alibaba, back in 1999, Ma didn't know anything about marketing, tech or financing. His main work experience had been as an English teacher. But he was able to turn the leadership of Alibaba into a collective force. "I chose my students," he explains. "And most of my time was spent identifying and cultivating their talents."

"With a team you can do something much better," he says, however brilliant an individual you are.

Teaching and mentoring are among the many things Jack Ma has become famous for, and young people are the lifeblood of his organization. "Newcomers are stronger than us in knowledge, capabilities and skills," he says. "Once we give them time, they will give us new success."

Be the honey badger

"This animal is fearless. He doesn't care who his opponent is. Just give him the time and location and he'll be there to fight. That's the kind of spirit that should be deep-rooted in an entrepreneur."

Honey badger is also the name Ma gave to his new chip company, Ping-Tou-Ge.

"To be the honey badger in your life - this is the essence of education," he explains. "Being you, not being Jack Ma. And don't imitate anybody. Just be yourself. I think that's very important."

Learn from the greats

Get out and meet people, and learn from them, advises Ma. He draws on his own experience: "For me, living here on this planet is an opportunity for me to know people of all varieties: good people, bad people, great people. And that is my nutrition."

"For my university and for entrepreneurs, the reason we are there is because we need to know about other people. But more importantly, we need to know about ourselves. We need to know how imperative it is to learn from the great people."

Mind your manners

There's still a vast cultural divide between Chinese and Western businesses, says Ma. And for both sides, there's a lot to learn about each other.

"China emphasizes that harmony gives you fortune. And in Western culture, competition makes you better," explains Ma. "But without the communication or respect and appreciation of others, you only have trouble and conflict on your hands."

"Westerners need to know China focuses on wisdom, but the Western world focuses on knowledge."

Don't focus on things that are hot

Startup founders, especially the young ones, tend to be easily distracted with current trends. The truth is, entrepreneur should focus and believe in his initial plans instead of just following what is hot nowadays. One reason why Alibaba succeeded was that the internet was not yet ubiquitous, Ma said.

"E-commerce was so cold. Nobody believed in it, but we believed in it. We didn't care what other people said. We thought it had a future, we thought it would help people, so we started."

"When everybody says yes, there's no chance for you – so be unique. Use your mind, think why you can do better, why you can do different, why you can last for 10 years while the other people can only last for one year," Ma said.

Great entrepreneur is always optimistic

It is crucial for entrepreneur to keep thinking positively towards everything. That being said, Ma suggested startup founder to get those negative thoughts out of their head because an entrepreneur should always be optimistic.

"You should be optimistic. Always optimistic. A great entrepreneur is optimistic for the future. And you have to ask what problem you can solve, and how you solve it is different from the others," he said.

One way to boost your optimism is by asking yourself why you can do better than everyone else in doing the same thing, added Ma.

See beyond your circumstances.

No matter what your current condition, how or where you grew up, or what education or training you feel you lack, you can be successful in your chosen endeavor. It is spirit, fortitude, and hardiness that matter more than where you start.

20

Elon Musk

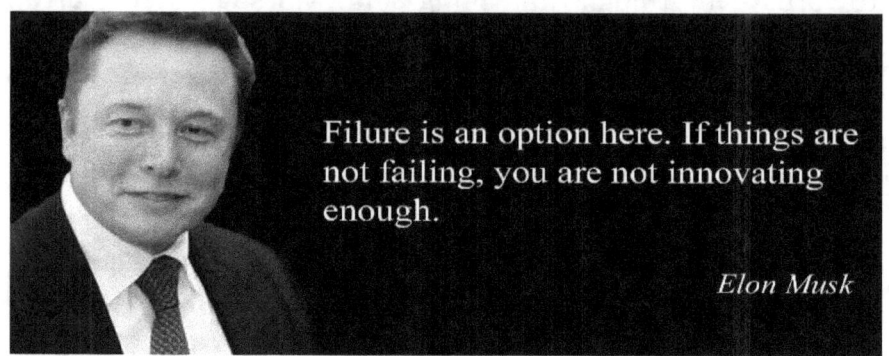

> Filure is an option here. If things are not failing, you are not innovating enough.
>
> *Elon Musk*

Biography

Elon Reeve Musk FRS (born June 28, 1971) is an engineer, industrial designer, technology entrepreneur and philanthropist. He is a citizen of South Africa, the United States (where he has lived most of his life and currently resides), and Canada. He is the founder, CEO and chief engineer/designer of SpaceX; co-founder, CEO and product architect of Tesla, Inc.; founder of The Boring Company;co-founder of Neuralink; and co-founder and initial co-chairman of OpenAI. He was elected a Fellow of the Royal Society (FRS) in 2018. In December 2016, he was ranked 21st on the Forbes list of The World's Most Powerful People,[14] and was ranked joint-first on the Forbes list of the Most Innovative Leaders of 2019. As of May 2020, he has a net worth of $36.5 billion and is listed by Forbes as the 31st-richest person in the world.He is the longest tenured CEO of any automotive manufacturer globally.

Born and raised in Pretoria, South Africa, Musk briefly attended the University of Pretoria before moving to Canada when he was 17 to attend Queen's University. He transferred to the University of Pennsylvania two years later, where he received a bachelor's degree in economics from the Wharton School and a bachelor's degree in physics from the College of Arts and Sciences. He began a Ph.D. in applied physics and material sciences at Stanford University in 1995 but dropped out after two days to pursue a business career. He subsequently co-founded (with his brother Kimbal) Zip2, a web software company, which was acquired by Compaq for $340 million in 1999. Musk then founded X.com, an online bank. It merged with Confinity in 2000, which had launched PayPal the previous year and was subsequently bought by eBay for $1.5 billion in October 2002.

SpaceX Demo-1 Preflight

In May 2002, Musk founded SpaceX, an aerospace manufacturer and space transport services company, of which he is CEO and lead designer. He joined Tesla Motors, Inc. (now Tesla, Inc.), an electric vehicle manufacturer, in 2004, the year after it was founded, and became its CEO and product architect. In 2006, he inspired the creation of SolarCity, a solar energy services company (now a subsidiary of Tesla). In 2015, Musk co-founded OpenAI, a nonprofit research company that aims to promote friendly artificial intelligence. In July 2016, he co-founded Neuralink, a neurotechnology company focused on developing brain–computer interfaces. In December 2016, Musk founded The Boring Company, an infrastructure and tunnel construction company focused on tunnels optimized for electric vehicles.

Apart from Tesla, Musk is not an investor in the stock market. In addition to his primary business pursuits, Musk has envisioned a high-speed transportation system known as the Hyperloop, and has proposed a vertical take-off and landing supersonic jet electric aircraft with electric fan propulsion, known as the Musk electric jet.Musk has said the goals of SpaceX, Tesla, and SolarCity revolve around his vision to "change the world and help humanity". His goals include reducing global warming through sustainable energy production and consumption, and reducing the risk of human extinction by establishing a human colony on Mars

Blueprint

Prepare for Disappointment

As with every startup, Elon Musk has faced inumerous challenges on the road to success, but he always cites a certain threshold for pain as being one of his major strengths. That is to say, Musk will often advise entrepreneurs and startups to expect pain and uncertainty at every turn.

In fact, Elon once described starting a company to "eating glass and staring into the abyss". It may sound rather negative but the truth is, this open minded approach is largely responsible for how he managed to pull through all the hard times.

Focus on Quality

I'd say stay very focused on the quality of the product. People get really wrapped up in all sorts of esoteric notions of how to manage etc., [but] I think people should get much more focused on the product itself – how do you make the product incredibly compelling to a customer – just become maniacally focused on building it better. – Elon Musk

Multitask

In the present day scenario, in addition to being a hard worker, you should also be a smart worker. The only way to achieve this is through multitasking and to juggle betweeen your priorities.

Right now, a business owner cannot afford to take his time to complete a job and move on to the next. Where time is money; every second that a person uses to multi-task can contribute towards to the general growth of his company in the long run.

Sacrifices Need To Be Made

Your start of an entrepreneurship journey is like delivering a baby. You need to nurture it, feed it and guide it to enable it to stand on its own.

You have to be at the core of the journey throughout and naturally, you cannot do that unless you are willing to make certain sacrifices of your own. Any business requires a certain amount of sacrifice and higher the goals are, the higher the sacrifices. Needless to say, Elon's success was not achieved without a string of sacrifices. Being the founder of not one but two billion dollar companies would certainly have its toll.

Keep The Bigger Picture In Mind

"One bit of advice: it is important to view knowledge as sort of a semantic tree – make sure you understand the fundamental principles like the trunk and big branches, before you get into the leaves/details or there is nothing for them to hang on to."

Think About Yourself Critically

"Accurate self analysis. It's difficult to do so, since you're too close to yourself by definition. People do not think critically enough. People assume too many things to be true without sufficient basis in that belief, so it's very important that people closely analyze what is supposed to be true, and build it up, analyze things by the first principles, not by analogy or convention, which is actually what most people do, that makes it difficult to gain insight as to how things can be bettered. In any argument or train of thinking, you want to make sure that the underlying premises are valid and applicable, and how the conclusion reached is necessarily driven by the underlying premises and the interconnection between those premises. It's the foundation of rational thought. "

Don't Fear Taking Risks

"People tend to over-weigh risks on a personal level. It's one thing if you've got a mortgage to pay and kids to support, so that if you were to deviate from your job, well, how are you going to feed your family and pay the rent? That's understandable, but let's say you're young and you're just coming out of college, what are your risks? You're not going to starve, certainly not in any kind of modern economy. It's so easy to earn enough money just to live somewhere and eat food. Very easy to do. So I don't know what they're afraid of. Mostly afraid of failure, I think, but people should be less risk averse, when there's not much at risk."

Hire The Right People

An alleged copy of Tesla's "Anti-Handbook Handbook" for new hires was leaked recently. It reflected the high standards that Musk holds up to Tesla's new hires:

"We want to surround ourselves with people driven to do the right things and act with integrity even when no one is looking," it states, followed by the warning that, "If this isn't you, you'll be more successful somewhere else. We don't mean to sound harsh; it's just the truth."

The main theme behind the handbook seems to be ideal that Musk holds to every employee: as invested in Tesla as Musk is. Tesla hires people not based on their resume but skills. If you are a Tesla employee, you are expected to do everything in your power to give your best performance. That includes directly reaching out to Musk to share any new ideas and knowledge. While top employees will certainly be with you during your highs, you need dedicated employees to ride out the lows. And that's what Tesla does perfectly.

Look For Problem Areas

People like to actively complain about things. Not Elon Musk. When Musk grew frustrated about the traffic problems that he faced, he started The Boring Company. The Boring Company aims to solve the traffic congestion problem by building a tunnel system.

To become a successful entrepreneur, find problems that need to be solved. Seeking out problems that need to be solved is a great way to find ideas about problems that people actually need some solution to.

21

Mark Zuckerberg

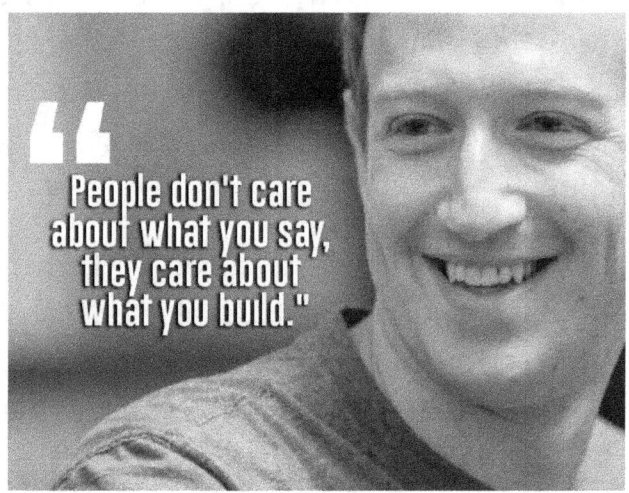

Biography

Mark Elliot Zuckerberg born May 14, 1984) is an American internet entrepreneur and philanthropist. He is known for co-founding Facebook, Inc. and serves as its chairman, chief executive officer, and controlling shareholder. He also co-founded and is a board member of the solar sail spacecraft development project Breakthrough Starshot.

Born in White Plains, New York, Zuckerberg attended Harvard University, where he launched the Facebook social networking service from his dormitory room on February 4, 2004, with college roommates Eduardo Saverin, Andrew

McCollum, Dustin Moskovitz, and Chris Hughes. Originally launched to select college campuses, the site expanded rapidly and eventually beyond colleges, reaching one billion users by 2012. Zuckerberg took the company public in May 2012 with majority shares. His net worth is estimated to be nearly $54 billion as of March 2020. In 2007, at age 23, he became the world's youngest self-made billionaire. As of 2019, he is the only person under 50 in the Forbes ten richest people list, and the only one under 40 in the Top 20 Billionaires list.

Since 2010, Time magazine has named Zuckerberg among the 100 wealthiest and most influential people in the world as a part of its Person of the Year award. In December 2016, Zuckerberg was ranked 10th on Forbes list of The World's Most Powerful People.

On February 4, 2004, Zuckerberg launched Facebook from his Harvard dormitory room. An earlier inspiration for Facebook may have come from Phillips Exeter Academy, the prep school from which Zuckerberg graduated in 2002. It published its own student directory, "The Photo Address Book", which students referred to as "The Facebook". Such photo directories were an important part of the student social experience at many private schools. With them, students were able to list attributes such as their class years, their friends, and their telephone numbers.

Once at college, Zuckerberg's Facebook started off as just a "Harvard thing" until Zuckerberg decided to spread it to other schools, enlisting the help of roommate Dustin Moskovitz. They began with Columbia University, New York University, Stanford, Dartmouth, Cornell, University of Pennsylvania, Brown, and Yale.[41] Samyr Laine, a triple jumper representing Haiti at the 2012 Summer Olympics, shared a room with Zuckerberg during Facebook's founding. "Mark was clearly on to great things," said Laine, who was Facebook's fourteenth user.

Zuckerberg, Moskovitz and some friends moved to Palo Alto, California in Silicon Valley where they leased a small house that served as an office. Over the summer, Zuckerberg met Peter Thiel, who invested in the company. They got their first office in mid-2004. According to Zuckerberg, the group planned to return to Harvard, but eventually decided to remain in California. They had already turned down offers by major corporations to buy the company. In an interview in 2007, Zuckerberg explained his reasoning: "It's not because of the amount of money. For me and my colleagues, the most important thing is that we create an open information flow for people. Having media corporations owned by conglomerates is just not an attractive idea to me."

He restated these goals to Wired magazine in 2010: "The thing I really care about is the mission, making the world open." Earlier, in April 2009, Zuckerberg sought the advice of former Netscape CFO Peter Currie about financing strategies for Facebook. On July 21, 2010, Zuckerberg reported that the company reached the 500 million-user mark. When asked whether Facebook could earn more income from advertising as a result of its phenomenal growth, he explained:

I guess we could ... If you look at how much of our page is taken up with ads compared to the average search query. The average for us is a little less than 10 percent of the pages and the average for search is about 20 percent taken up with ads ... That's the simplest thing we could do. But we aren't like that. We make enough money. Right, I mean, we are keeping things running; we are growing at the rate we want to.

Blueprint

Do it for you

With any career move or new business idea, there is no guarantee that it's going to work out. Chances are, you will see very few results at the beginning, and you may working on and believing in your vision alone for a long time. Because of this, Mark Zuckerberg advises that you should find and idea you're passionate about and launch the project for yourself.

Make innovation your focus

Your motivation is a big part of the success of your idea. If you are creating an IT startup with the intention of just making money or being important, you are not going to be fully committed to the project and are probably doing it for the wrong reasons. Instead, Zuckerberg says you should focus on coming up with a new solution to a particular problem, and it will evolve from there.

"I always think that you should start with the problem that you're trying to solve in the world and not start with deciding that you want to build a company," he said to Altman.

Think long term

When you're developing your startup, it's easy to get caught up with short term goals. But jumping prematurely on an opportunity could cause you to miss out on something better later down the track. This was the challenge for Zuckerberg when Yahoo offered him $1 billion for Facebook. He turned it down, and was able to become the multi-billion dollar company we know today.

Surround yourself with the right people

Finally, Mark Zuckerberg is well known for his leadership ability, and a big part of this is hiring the right team to help the business reach its goals. No one can do everything on their own, and once your tech startup has become established, you need to know when it's time to bring on more staff to enable it to expand further. Whether you are looking to fill app developer roles or someone to code your new software, you should surround yourself with the highest quality talent that is going to be committed to achieving your vision for the future.

Have a high purpose

Zuckerberg says that he never intended to start Facebook as a company. According to him, he just wanted it personally to satisfy a global need to connect. His social mission has always been "to make the world more open and connected". In one of his letters to the shareholders, Zuckerberg wrote:

"Facebook was not originally created to be a company. It was built to accomplish a social mission – to make the world more open and connected."

Test the Market

Before implementing his website Facebook, he set up a short lived Facemash, a Harvard-specific photo rating site that functioned like HotOrNot.com but employed photographs taken from Harvard's online Facebook. After its success, in February, 2004, he commenced "The Facebook". It included aims of Facemash combined with the diverse aspects of social networking sites like Myspace (Inspiring Stories from Famous Entrepreneurs – Mark Zuckerberg, 2010). In the first m nth of its launch more than 50% undergraduate population of Harvard were registered with this service. After attaining success in initial months, he planned to expand his service that every entrepreneur performs who have all skills and risk taking ability. In March 2004, he expanded Facebook to Stanford, Columbia, and Yale. This expansion of the website was extended as it also unfolded to all Ivy League and Boston area schools. Subsequently, it was open to most of the Canada and U.S. universities (Mark Zuckerberg, 2010).

Financial Backing

When Mark Zuckerberg started Facebook it was just for the students of Harvard University. When it attained immense popularity in a short time period, Zuckerberg involved his friends and fellow students Dustin Moskovitz, Chris Hughes, Eduardo Saverin and Andrew McCollum to help him in its establishment (Today's Whiz Kid Mark Zuckerberg, n.d.). In a short duration, it was opened for other university students of Boston area. Afterwards, he also opened membership for all American universities and high school students.

After some time, Zuckerberg and Moskovitz decided to move the operations of Facebook's to Palo Alto, California. At there, they started an office throughout the summer of 2004. They received financial backing from PayPal co-founder Peter Theil. In September 2006, the site that was not recognized as Facebook was unfolded for the general public. This site was allowed to be used by anyone who is older than 13 years (Kaushik, 2009). With the help of financial backing, Mark Zuckerberg was able to start his office and company.

With his all-inclusive approach towards his dream, he become able in receiving financial backing that is essential as without this it is not possible for an individual to start a company. With the support of PayPal co-founder in present, the company has become able in involving 200 million active users (Daft & Lane, 2009). With this increasing number of active users this social networking website of Mark has become second most popular online social network after MySpace.

Be Passionate About What You Do

When you closely scrutinize the lives of some of the most successful entrepreneurs over the globe, you will notice a common trait in all of them. They are passionate about what they do. The same passion has enabled Facebook to innovate continuously and overcome every obstacle that came its way. It is that same passion which helped our Facebook prodigy reject multitudes of buyout offers, even in the face of adversity. Donald Trump sums it up brilliantly when he said, "Without passion, you don't have energy, and without energy you have nothing."

Stay in Learning Mode All the Time

It is the desire to learn new things that led to the creation of Facebook. From an early age, Mark Zuckerberg had a predilection for computers and programming. He even developed a program called ZuckNet to connect his father's home and office computers at the tender age of 11. He made games out of his friend's drawings and learned many different languages along the way. The list goes on and on. Despite having touched the upper Echelon in his niche, he still signs up for courses to stay abreast of the latest developments in the world of technology.

Know what you want to build

According to Zuckerberg, one of the most important aspects of determining a company's success is to know what it is trying to accomplish. He says that entrepreneurs should pinpoint the problem they want their business to solve in order to give it direction and drive it forward with a vision. There is little point in starting a company if you don't know what the point to it is, so you need to decide on this before you take any other steps.

If you want to build something great, you should focus on what the change is that you want to make in the world. I see too many entrepreneurs who decide that they want to start a company before they actually know what it is they want to build. To me, that seems backwards.

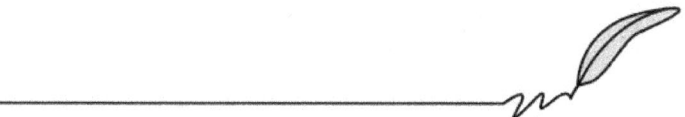

www.ingramcontent.com/pod-product-compliance
Lightning Source LLC
Chambersburg PA
CBHW071351210526
45465CB00001B/56